LOVE YOURSELF, LOVE YOUR LIFE

LOVE YOURSELF, LOVE YOUR LIFE

*Unleash Your Inner Power to
Love, Heal, Blossom and Create
the Life of Your Dreams*

GAIL TAYLOR-SMITH

Love Yourself, Love Your Life © Copyright 2025 Gail Taylor-Smith

All rights reserved. No part of this publication may be reproduced, distributed or transmitted in any form or by any means, including photocopying, recording, or other electronic or mechanical methods, without the prior written permission of the publisher, except in the case of brief quotations embodied in critical reviews and certain other noncommercial uses permitted by copyright law.

Although the author and publisher have made every effort to ensure that the information in this book was correct at press time, the author and publisher do not assume and hereby disclaim any liability to any party for any loss, damage, or disruption caused by errors or omissions, whether such errors or omissions result from negligence, accident, or any other cause.

Adherence to all applicable laws and regulations, including international, federal, state and local governing professional licensing, business practices, advertising, and all other aspects of doing business in the US, Canada or any other jurisdiction is the sole responsibility of the reader and consumer.

Neither the author nor the publisher assumes any responsibility or liability whatsoever on behalf of the consumer or reader of this material. Any perceived slight of any individual or organization is purely unintentional.

The resources in this book are provided for informational purposes only and should not be used to replace the specialized training and professional judgment of a health care or mental health care professional.

Neither the author nor the publisher can be held responsible for the use of the information provided within this book. Please always consult a trained professional before making any decision regarding treatment of yourself or others.

For more information, email heartofdog@hotmail.com

ISBN: 979-8-89694-115-6 Paperback
ISBN: 979-8-89694-114-9 eBook

Disclaimer: This book is intended for informational purposes only. The content provided here is not intended as medical advice, diagnosis, or treatment. Readers should not rely on this information as a substitute for professional medical care by a physician or mental health professional. The author and publisher are not responsible for any adverse effects or outcomes resulting from the use or application of the information provided in this book. Always consult a qualified healthcare provider with questions regarding any medical condition or treatment and before beginning any new exercise, nutrition, or lifestyle program. Individual results may vary, and no guarantees of specific outcomes are made by this author, nor are any liabilities being assumed. The reader is responsible for his or her own actions.

Dedication

To my wonderful mother, who always believed in me and encouraged me to follow my dreams. Thank you for your sacrifices, love, and support, which have meant everything to me. I am so grateful to have you in my life.

For my beloved rescued fur babies, Bella, Layla, and Tiger, who have brought me an abundance of joy and helped me to unleash my inner powers through their unconditional love and passion.

With love and gratitude to Dr Sue Morter and the Energy Codes Community for igniting my creativity and greater love, inspiring me to create this book and share your magnificence.

The transformative impact you have provided through The Morter Institute has unlocked my creator powers.

Contents

Dedication 5
Introduction 11
Chapter 1: Understanding Your Current Mindset 21
    Limiting Beliefs 22
    Past Experiences 28
    Limiting Beliefs and Past Experiences Exercise 33
    Next Steps 36
Chapter 2: The Power Inside - Shifting Your Perspective ... 37
    Shifting from Being Externally Focused to Internally Focused 39
    Practice: Shifting from Externally Focused to Internally Focused .. 42
    Overcoming Inner Child Wounds 44
    Overcoming Inner Child Wounds Exercise 54
    Next Steps 57
Chapter 3: The Power of Intention - Setting
             Intentions for What You Truly Desire 59
    Setting Intentions Exercise 65
    Next Steps 69
Chapter 4: Power of Inspired Action 70
    What is an inspired action? 73
    Imagine Stepping out of Your Comfort Zone 75
    Taking Inspired Action Exercise 77
    Next Steps 80

Chapter 5: Power of Love, Part 1 -
         Cultivating Self-Love and Self-Care 81
  Self-Love 83
  Self-Care 87
  Possible Self-Care and Self-Love Expressions 89
  Self-Love and Self-Care Exercise 94
  Next Steps 97

Chapter 6: The Power Of Music and Sound 99
  Power of Music and Sound - Focus 100
  Power of Music and Sound – Physical and Emotional Healing ...103
  Power of Music and Sound – Connection 107
  Power of Music and Sound Exercise 110
  Next Steps 113

Chapter 7: Power of Intuition - Listening to Your
         Intuitive Inner Voice 114
  Power of Intuition- Listening to Your Intuitive Inner Voice Exercise 120
  Next Steps 122

Chapter 8: Power of Love, Part 2 - Embracing
         Love and Passion 124
  Love is the Answer, the Secret Power - The Key to Unlock Your Heart 125
  Passion in Your Life 131
  Embracing Love and Passion Exercise 134
  Next Steps 138

Chapter 9: Unleash Your Inner Powers - Love,
         Heal, Blossom and Create the Life of
         Your Dreams 140
  Reflection 141
  The Six Creator Powers 144
  Next Steps 150

References and Resources 155
Acknowledgments 157
About the Author 161

Introduction

Imagine having the power to love, heal, blossom and create the life of your dreams. Are you ready to unleash your inner power and unlock your ability to be the creator of your destiny?

Do you feel that self-love is missing in your life? Have you heard your mind saying or felt that you are not good enough or not worthy, not appreciated, not respected, not valued, or not loved either at work or in your personal life? Perhaps it just feels like there is a void, an empty space, inside of you and you don't know why or what you can do to fill it.

Have you ever had the feeling that you were not yet living to your highest potential? Perhaps it manifested as not connecting with your mission, purpose, passion, or true desires. Has there been a time when you felt challenged to create changes to your life circumstances, resulting in fear, anger, or sadness? Do you want to have more control of your life, instead of being a mere victim of circumstances?

If you said "Yes" to any of these questions, then this book is for you!

There was a time in my life where I said "Yes" to all those questions.

Love Yourself, Love Your Life will solve your problems by providing solutions, proven techniques to overcome what's holding you back. You will learn how to truly love yourself and create a life that you love living! In this book, I will show you how loving yourself is the key to unlocking your power. The practical and easy to use tools presented in this book will transform your life from where you are now to one filled with love, joy and abundance. You will experience emotional and physical healing because you will be taking inspired action in alignment with your heart's desire and living to your fullest potential, no longer the victim reacting to your external circumstances. When you change the way you think, feel and behave, you unlock your power to blossom and be the creator of your life from the inside out.

Since the day I was born, trying to crawl in the hospital bed after birth, it was my destiny to create change. I have always been and always will be a creator. It was meant to be that I would be successful at changing the patterns associated with the external circumstances I was born into and the resultant programming my mind received. The programming that said I wasn't good enough or worthy, that I was a victim of my circumstances. Yes, there were obstacles and challenges to be overcome, both physically and emotionally. Somehow I intuitively knew at a very young age that I was responsible for creating the change I wanted and needed to see. I knew in my heart and soul that I was here to achieve a greater purpose in my life.

In spite of my programming, I transformed myself from being a victim to the creator of my life. After many years of hard work and sacrifice, I had my dream—an ocean view office as an Executive at a research laboratory, creating technologies for future Aerospace and Automotive systems. Then came the *revelation*—there was still something that was *missing* in my life. I wasn't feeling love, not feeling valued at work or in my personal life. The sciatic pain was getting worse in my right leg. I started to get sinus infections more frequently. There was an empty space inside that needed to be filled. What was I missing? What was my real mission and purpose in this life? How would I achieve my highest potential? What was the change I needed to create now?

While I had thrived on creating change my entire life and there were many powerful tools I had already discovered, I didn't know the answer. Instead of knowing what was next, there was just a big black void! A total lack of inspiration about what was next on my journey through life. My inner voice said it was time to look deeper inside myself to find the answers. Instead of doing research for work, my life became a research project. I asked myself: What am I missing?

I became fascinated with neuroscience and quantum physics. I learned that my thoughts created my reality. I became curious about how I could change the thought patterns created by the programming I received as a child. Through the actions I had taken, I had created the change needed to achieve much greater success than anyone else in my family had ever dreamed of achieving. By looking deeper inside I had a revelation - I was still programmed to be the victim.

At some level, I didn't feel worthy or good enough, not deserving. I still lived with the fear of not having or being enough. Truth was, I didn't love myself enough. Unconditional love for myself was what was needed to shift from being the victim to the creator of my life.

It was time to take responsibility for achieving my destiny of love, abundance and joy. I realized that was what I truly desired and deserved. I needed to find practical tools that would allow me to unlock the power inside of me to live at my highest potential, to become the creator of my life from the inside out. By becoming the creator of my life, I could reclaim my power from the people and circumstances around me.

Just as I did in my career as an engineer, I embarked on a research project with the intention of reclaiming my power. My dilemma when I started my research project was that there were so many teachers and tools to choose from, all claiming to create the change I needed. Each one had a unique approach, and each one cost both time and money, some more than others. My intention was to discover practical tools that created sustainable change with grace and ease. Many of the teachers whose work I engaged with were not worth the time and money spent.

After experimenting with many different approaches, I learned which resulted in the biggest evolutionary impacts in my life. My passion in writing this book is to share the results of my experiences and research with you. With this knowledge, you can transform your life for less money and at an accelerated pace - in weeks to months, instead of years! Through my years of research, I discovered the tools that allowed me to sustainably unleash the power inside of my heart, the power of love. I've learned that love transmutes and transforms all that is not love, empowering you to be the creator of a life in which you love yourself and your life.

The tools I will share in this book are the ones I found to be the most practical and easy to use. They have created sustainable transformation in my life by consistently creating more love, joy and abundance in my life! I have overcome the victim programming and reactivity. I am good enough! I have enough! I love myself and my life!

The real blessing, or icing on the cake, is that with the tools I will share, I have experienced significant emotional and physical healing. Where I used to live in constant pain in my sciatic nerve due to scoliosis, I am now pain free. In general, I have found that I heal from physical injuries much more quickly and easily. I happily love myself unconditionally, no longer a victim of my external circumstances frustrated and sad. In fact, I am happy to say that I am the healthiest I have ever been in my life, from the inside out, and without medication!

Are you ready to unlock the power of your heart to blossom by creating a life filled with love, abundance, and joy? Are you ready to heal emotionally and physically?

The reality is that change is constant and creates vitality. Everything that will happen or has happened in your life happened for a reason—a good reason. Think about a time when something good magically appeared in your life because of a change that intentionally or unintentionally happened to you. I am a change agent. My entire life story is about accepting or creating change. You have the ability to create the change you want to see in your life. If you desire it, if you are passionate about it, you can make it so! The truth is that your thoughts create your reality.

You have so much more control over the outcomes in your life than you think you do. I know because I have been where you are now. What I have learned on my journey is that my mind was controlling everything based upon the programming I had received as a child. My true powers were either hidden inside of me or given away to other people. When you reclaim your power, you are in control of your destiny. You are energy in motion, always changing and evolving in alignment with your highest potential. Why not be the creator of the change rather than reacting to or being the victim of the changes that happen to you? Within you, you have the power and freedom to create a life of abundance for yourself, to live a life that you love living and to be surrounded by the people and places that bring you joy and happiness.

What are you waiting for? You can do this! It was meant to be! It's your destiny! Unlock your power as the creator of your life!

You deserve to have love, joy and abundance! You don't need to be the victim trying to survive anymore. I know because I changed my destiny using the approaches I will share in this book. All you need to do is overcome your "programming." Yes, that's right. Your mind has been programmed since the moment you entered your mother's womb. What I mean by programming is similar to how the software in your computer, cell phone, or car is programmed to respond in certain ways based upon the external inputs or prompts they receive.

The key to unlocking the creator powers inside you is *Love*! *Love* is the answer to all your challenges—self-love, and embracing unconditional love for others. My only wish is that I would have realized this secret when I was younger. I was always worried about pleasing others, constantly looking for approval and appreciation from the people at work or my significant other. I would always compare myself to others and be worried about what other people thought about me. Never feeling good enough or worthy. I hated my body—I was too fat, my feet were too big, my boobs were too small.

How could it be so simple yet transformative as self-love and unconditional love? Now I know the truth that love is the secret weapon. I guess at an intuitive level I always knew it was true. As I reflect on the past, it was always a part of who I was and how I showed up as a leader at work. When I needed to write a poem in junior high French class, it was about love being the key.

My intention and inspiration in creating this book is to provide practical tools and resources to help others discover that love is the answer through the **_Six Creator Powers_**. Based upon my experience researching and experimenting with a wide range of tools over many years, I discovered these six powers created a framework in which I could live to my highest potential. By embracing and unlocking these six powers you will be empowered to express your magnificence and live your highest purpose.

Not only am I living a life filled with joy and love, these tools have greatly enhanced my emotional and physical well being. Before I unleashed and embraced my **_Six Creator Powers_**, I lived in constant pain from scoliosis induced lower back issues, my kidney function was declining, and my immune system was weak due to high stress levels. With these tools, I am happy, healthy and pain free from the inside out.

These are the **_Six Creator Powers_** I will share with you in this book:

First, the **_Power Inside,_** by **_shifting your focus from your external environment to internal._** This book will inspire you to take full responsibility for your life. By embracing an internal locus of control, you can move from being a victim of your circumstances to being the creator and architect of your own destiny. Your past experiences and limiting beliefs do not control you and do not determine your future, unless you let them. The most important time to be present in is the present moment, the infinite now where infinite possibilities exist. This requires stepping out of your comfort zone and letting go of past experiences and inner child reactivity. Change your inner world, and your outer world will change too!

Second, the **_Power of Intention_** You will chart a course to your innermost desires, goals and intentions, creating a new version of you that is based upon the **Power Inside**! By ***creating intentions*** for your life from the Power Inside, you become the creator of your life. It requires changing your paradigm and shifting to a more empowered and intentional mindset, shifting your life from external validation to internal fulfillment. By embracing the feelings your heart desires, you can create a new reality filled with an abundance of love and joy.

Third, the **Power of Music and Sound**. ***Tuning into*** the **Power of Music and Sound** is a practical tool that will help you connect with your heart, your inner voice, your body, and with other people. ***Listening and moving to music*** has been shown to improve emotional and physical wellbeing by reducing stress and supporting the body in healing. Music can help you to achieve a state of flow where you are connected to a steady stream of divine intelligence.

Fourth, the **Power of Intuition**. ***Listening*** to your ***intuitive inner voice*** in your daily routine to help you make the internal shift you need, and make decisions with grace and ease, to live an empowered life that you love living! There is so much information available to you inside yourself if you listen to the voice in your heart and gut. They know what is in your highest good.

Fifth, the **Power of Inspired Action. *Taking inspired action aligned with your intuitive inner voice and passions*** helps you create a life filled with meaning and deep satisfaction. By fostering a sense of curiosity and using your imagination, you'll explore new opportunities and realize your untapped potential. You'll discover that you can step out of your comfort zone and not only survive, but thrive!

Sixth, and most importantly, the **Power of Love**! ***Being heart-centered in love in all that you do*** every day, personally and professionally. Love is the answer! Love is the key to unlocking your heart. It will transform your life! Loving your body because it is beautiful. Loving your inner child to overcome reactivity. Loving and caring for yourself unconditionally. Listening to your loving heart by listening to your intuitive inner voice. Loving your mind when it tells you stories. Loving yourself by forgiving yourself for anything you did or didn't do, said or didn't say. Loving yourself and others by not judging.

I was born into an environment in which no one in my family had ever been to college. My parents had an 8th grade education. We lived in constant fear of not having enough money. Based upon my environment, I was destined to a life of lack unless I was the one to change the pattern and the story. If that wasn't challenging enough, I chose to become an engineer and face the challenges of working in a male dominated environment. In this book, I share how I successfully shifted my life from lack to abundance, how I successfully overcame the covert obstacles of discrimination to become an Advanced Technology Development Executive in a large corporation. I will share the practical tools that I used to change the patterns. You can do it too!

The first step in your journey to a new you is understanding your current mindset. You can't shift your reality without first becoming aware of and accepting the truth about who you are now. Be honest with yourself. You deserve to honor and trust yourself. Remember the key to unlocking your power is love, and that means loving yourself unconditionally and fully embracing the truth of who you are now. Let the journey begin!

Chapter I

Understanding Your Current Mindset

> *"I was exhilarated by the new realization that I could change the character of my life by changing my beliefs. I was instantly energized because I realized that there was a science-based path that would take me from my job as a perennial "victim" to my new position as "co-creator" of my destiny."*
>
> – BRUCE H. LIPTON, PHD

Having been trained as an engineer, when I discovered Bruce Lipton early in my journey, I was drawn to the scientific basis of his teachings. Specifically, on his website he references the quantum physics principles I became passionate about studying. Quantum physics has shown that your experiences in the physical world are deeply connected to the inner workings of your mind. This quote gave me hope and a different perspective. It provided the seed of possibility in my mind that I really could shift my path from being the victim to the creator of my life.

As Bruce Lipton said in his quote, you each have the power within you to change your mindset, to change the programming and beliefs that you received as children. My revelation? My mind already had evidence that this was true. Unlike my parents, or any of my cousins or their parents, I was the first person in my family to graduate from college. Yes, I had already overcome some of the programming I received as a child. Within me was the power to choose, to be the creator of my destiny. My choice was to let go of limiting beliefs and reprogram my mind to become the creator of my life. This means you too have the power to choose to become whatever you want as creator of your life, by shifting your mindset.

Your mindset is a set of beliefs that shape how you make sense of the world and yourself. It influences how you think, feel, and behave in any given situation. It means that what you believe about yourself impacts your success or failure, your lack or abundance. It can manifest in a number of different ways in your life. Change your beliefs and you can change your life!

Bottom line—are you living your life as a victim or as a creator? Are you living your life to your highest potential, realizing the abundance, love, and joy you deserve in all aspects of your life? To evolve into this life of abundance, love, and joy, you must first identify and tackle the beliefs that limit you.

Limiting Beliefs

I grew up in a family that had a "victim" mindset.

What I mean by a "victim" mindset is an unreasonable belief that one is always a victim, with a tendency to blame others and feel powerless. It is a mentality in which you do not take responsibility for what happens in your life because you feel that it is not under your control. You feel powerless to change your circumstances or the outcomes of your actions.

My Dad lost his Mom during the birth of his youngest brother when he was only five years old. His Dad quickly remarried to provide a "family" for the three boys. He grew up with a stepmother that never treated him like a real son. She had children from a prior marriage and two new children born with my grandfather. My Dad was forced to drop out of school in 8th grade to start earning money for his family to survive. He wasn't allowed to keep any of the money he earned. His parents took all of his earnings to use as they saw best to support the family, never showing gratitude or compassion for his contributions. As a result, he was the victim of his childhood circumstances, feeling unloved and abandoned. He never really learned how to express gratitude and love, except by hiding his feelings behind taunting words.

My Dad grew up in an environment where he felt he was the victim. Always being the victim is a limiting belief. Did you grow up in an environment with a prevalent victim mindset?

Limiting beliefs are perceptions and thoughts you have about yourself, others, and the world. These perceptions and thoughts are preventing you from doing something that you're actually quite capable of doing, even though you don't think you are! Telling yourself you are always the victim is a limiting belief!

To be able to shift your perspective by changing your beliefs, you first need to have awareness of your limiting beliefs. You need to take a hard look at yourself in the mirror and acknowledge the truth. These beliefs can be passed down from your parents or created in your childhood environment, as they were for me when I was a child.

My Mom started out as a good student in school, but then things changed. She dropped out of school after 8th grade. My sense based upon what she has subtly hinted at was that she was abused by her father. I can only imagine the feelings of shame, abandonment, and other emotional trauma that she must still feel. She was never able to release the pain by talking about it with anyone, even me, consequently becoming the perpetual victim.

What I have increasingly realized the more time I spend with my Mom is that she always felt like she was being punished. Whenever things didn't go as she desired, she would say it was because she was being punished. She felt unworthy or undeserving of happiness and abundance. Instead she was committed to being unhappy, worthy only of being the victim, being punished by being in lack. Never able to have what she truly desired. At the same time, she was always hiding her feelings deep inside, unwilling to take responsibility for them and instead letting her mind, her thoughts, control her.

My Mom was 18 when she married my 19 year old Dad, never having the opportunity to truly know herself and heal her wounds. She had me three years later when she was 21. My brother was born less than two years later. When I was a child, we barely had enough money to keep food on the table, often relying on food stamps. Growing up in this environment, I was unavoidably programmed into the "victim" mentality. I was programmed to blame others when things didn't go my way. I was afraid to speak what was in my thoughts, afraid to express my true feelings. I didn't feel good enough, or worthy, severely lacking in self-confidence. The childhood wounds were deeply embedded in my mind and in my body, creating many limiting beliefs.

In essence, a limiting belief is a story you tell yourself to keep you in your comfort zone. These beliefs prevent you from becoming who you are meant to be. They prevent you from living to your highest potential. These limiting beliefs become programmed into your subconscious mind, where they are more challenging to overcome. They have a negative impact on your life, creating fear and anxiety when you try to make changes in your life.

In my case, the limiting beliefs holding me back were: I'm not good enough; I need to get a perfect report card or I'm stupid; the other kids are better than me; I can't because the other kids will make fun of me or pick on me; I always get in trouble at school; I don't have enough money to get what I want; the teachers give too much homework and it's too hard for me. Bottom line—because of my limiting beliefs, I struggled to get good grades and fit in with the other kids at school.

All that being said, deep down I knew there had to be another answer. When I was 12 years old we moved from the east coast to the west coast to be closer to my Dad's family and a better job. Miraculously, I suddenly excelled at school, becoming an "A" student. I became the first person in my family to graduate from college with a Bachelor of Science in Engineering from the University of California, Los Angeles (UCLA), funding my education with financial aid and scholarships. Since my parents didn't have the money to send me to college, I was truly grateful and blessed to be able to leverage other people's money to obtain my degree. My parents and grandparents were so excited to attend my UCLA graduation ceremony!

With my degree in hand, I interviewed for an entry level Engineering position with multiple companies. Since I was a science fiction fan, my intuition told me to accept the offer as a Member of the Technical Staff at Hughes Space and Communications in El Segundo, CA. One of the benefits of accepting this position was it included an offer to complete a Master of Science degree in Electrical Engineering from the University of Southern California (USC) through the Hughes Fellowship program. The Hughes Fellowship program covered 100 percent of my graduate school tuition and book costs while I worked full time as an engineer. This was the only way I could afford graduate school, especially at USC. Two years later I graduated with my Master of Science degree in Electrical Engineering.

As an engineer, I discovered that I was surrounded by men! Women were less than 10 percent of the workforce. In the government program area in which I worked, it was less than 5 percent. When I moved into a leadership role for advanced technology development, there were less than 5 percent women. Due to my limiting beliefs, I always struggled with being able to speak up in meetings with my male superiors, not feeling worthy or good enough to be heard around men my Dad's age. It was a challenging environment where discrimination against a female in that role was predominantly covert.

Despite the challenges, I was able to work my way up to becoming a first level Executive within the Hughes culture. When Boeing purchased Hughes, the culture was very different. It was more political and less technology focused. I had reached the limit of living as the victim. My limiting beliefs sabotaged me. I felt that I wasn't good enough or worthy of attaining a higher position. I was never able to express myself or speak my truth confidently when in the presence of my superiors. I had no problem expressing myself with customers or the people that worked for me, just the people (men) above me in the corporate chain.

Just like my parents, I was in the victim mindset when it came to being able to achieve my highest potential. I blamed the people I reported to for not acknowledging my value and contributions. It was time to step out of my comfort zone once again and create a new beginning in another company. It was time to shift from being a victim to a creator by using the tools I will share in this book. In making this shift, I am now the creator of a life of abundance, love, and joy.

Ask yourself: *"What are the limiting beliefs in my current mindset?"*

Do you take responsibility for what happens to you, or do you have a tendency to blame others for what happens? If you blame others, you are perceiving yourself as the victim. Do you view challenges and change as learning opportunities for growth, or do you have a tendency to shy away from them? If you shy away from challenges and change, you may perceive that you are not worthy or not good enough to achieve the outcome. Do you feel or express gratitude for the blessings and abundance in your life, or find yourself comparing what you have to what others have?

If you often find yourself comparing yourself to others, you may have the limiting belief that others are more worthy or deserving than you. These are just a few of the questions you can consider when trying to understand your limiting beliefs.

Do you lack the confidence to fully express your magnificence? Are you hesitant to share your true feelings because you are afraid of how others will judge you? Commit yourself to making a shift from Victim to Creator and living to your highest potential! Commit yourself to shifting your mindset by understanding your limiting beliefs. Your limiting beliefs must be overcome to live to your highest potential in both your personal and professional life. As Bruce Lipton said, you can change the programming and become the co-creator of your destiny!

Many of your limiting beliefs were shaped by your past experiences, which we will explore next.

Past Experiences

Limiting beliefs isn't the only thing that can shape your mindset. Do you have past experiences that are impacting your current reality? Does your "monkey mind," the voice in your head that keeps you living in the past, keep telling you that you can't do something that you want to do now because of something that happened in your past? Your mind really does live in the past! Your mind has memories based upon, but not always *factually* representing, past experiences that can control your actions, thoughts, and feelings.

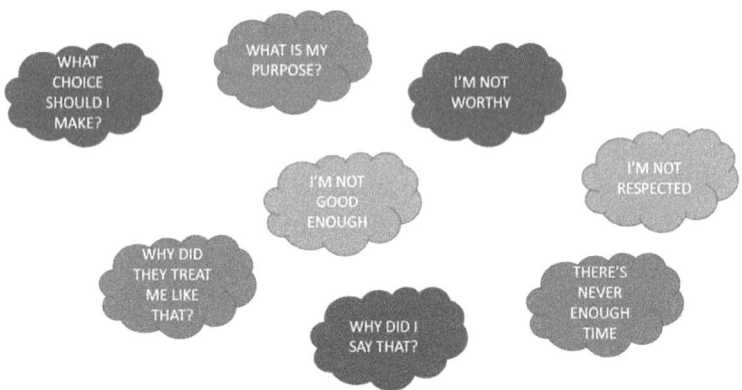

The Voice of Your 'Monkey Mind'

I'll share a couple of past experiences in my life to demonstrate my point.

When I was a child, sitting at the dinner table, being curious, I would attempt to engage in conversation with my family members. My Dad would yell at me for doing so: "*Children are to be seen, not heard. Shut up or you will get the paddle!*" The "paddle" was used on my behind when I was a "bad girl". I didn't want the paddle, so I quickly learned to stifle my expression.

Many years later when I was starting out as an engineer, in a meeting with all older men, guess what happened? I was afraid to speak up, afraid that I would get in trouble for expressing myself. If I did find the courage to speak up, I would blush with embarrassment as if I was doing something wrong. It was horrifying! I never overcame that past childhood experience until I became a Toastmaster, facing my fears to become a better speaker through weekly practice. Rebuilding the muscles, reprogramming my mind to have the required confidence. Shifting my perspective from not being good enough to being confident. Moving from victim to creator.

The second past example involves my first husband. Everything was beautiful at the beginning. Love, shared experiences, happiness. Then one year, it was time for our vacation to Hawaii over Valentine's Day. What could be more romantic? A couple of days before the trip my husband told me he wasn't going! What? Not going! Why? We had been planning the vacation for months. How could he suddenly bail on me, especially when it was over Valentine's Day? That was the first real sign I had that he was having an affair with someone. Or was it? I recalled there was also the time when I saw lipstick, which clearly wasn't mine, on a shirt he wore on a business trip.

When I confronted him, he lied and said there wasn't anyone else. There were more signs indicating that he was indeed having an affair, namely sexually transmitted diseases. Given that I was not having sex with anyone except him, yet contracted trichomoniasis (a parasite) and human papillomavirus (also known as genital warts), both of which can only be transmitted through sexual intercourse, it became evident that he was having sex with someone other than me. After my gynecologist told me he would need to be treated for the disease too, everything became crystal clear.

My limiting beliefs prevented me from taking action initially. I avoided the subject. I pretended to believe his lies and allowed him to gaslight me because I felt I didn't deserve better. I was in denial. It had to be my fault that he cheated. I wasn't good enough. I didn't deserve to be loved and respected. I felt rejected and hoped that things would improve. I worked even harder to please him, to make him happy by giving and loving more.

Things didn't improve. Over time there was a complete lack of intimacy in our relationship. This was the proverbial straw that broke the camel's back. It compelled me to step out of my comfort zone and my commitment to our marriage and leave him. My intuition said the affairs had to be true. I couldn't deny it any longer. It was time to listen to my intuition and accept the truth I had been afraid to believe. He broke my heart. I was devastated.

My heart, which already had a box around it to protect me, now had a fortress around it. My limiting beliefs were reconfirmed once again. I had allowed myself to make sacrifices for love. I never experienced the joy of being a mother because he didn't want kids. Now it was too late. His cheating on me confirmed that I wasn't good enough. I wasn't worthy of being loved by myself or anyone else. I didn't deserve pure and faithful love, hence there was no need to try again. And yes, this gave my mind more evidence that I was indeed the victim. My mind was more determined than ever to protect me by not allowing me to open my heart and "*love.*"

When I married my first husband, I had not yet learned to love myself. Based upon the programming from my Mom, I didn't feel worthy to *receive love* from myself. The only love I knew was *giving love* to others. I loved him. I opened and gave my heart to him completely. My love was completely *externally focused*. My sense of worth was based upon his feelings for me and how my friends and co-workers treated me. My parents never learned how to love themselves, and that was the only reality I knew. I have since learned the importance of loving myself and knowing that I am loved, no matter what my external circumstances would have me believe. I no longer fill the role of the victim by letting others take the power of my love for myself away from me. I allow myself to receive the love that I had previously only given to others.

Perhaps you have had similar emotional experiences in your past which your mind uses to protect you, thereby impacting your current reality. When you were born, your brain was not fully developed. As an infant and young child, your brain was a sponge collecting information from your environment, from your experiences, forming beliefs based on that information, creating patterns of behavior. The neural connections established in the brain based upon that information become a guide for you for the rest of your life, if you allow them to do so.

If you've had the opportunity to observe a child growing up then you know what I'm talking about. A child rapidly absorbs information from its environment at such a high rate that by age six, thousands of beliefs form in the child's mind. Just like a computer or cell phone is programmed to perform certain functions with software and firmware, the mind of a child is programmed through the neural connections in the brain, creating beliefs that help the child interact with the world.

Everything you have learned, from how to play with others, to how to read, to how to resolve conflicts, makes you who you are now, and to a large extent was created in your neural connections when you were a child. Every present-day experience of being cared for includes all your past experiences of being loved by others, all the way back to adolescence and childhood, no matter what your current age.

These past experiences are often associated with strong emotions. The emotions of rejection that I felt when my Dad told me I couldn't speak unless I was spoken to. The emotion of sadness when my first husband cheated on me with another woman. One happened as a child, the other as an adult. They both shaped who I became after the experience, influencing my thoughts and feelings in personal and professional relationships.

What are some of the past experiences that shaped you as a person, either as a child or an adult? What are some of the emotions that arise when you recall these experiences now?

While it is challenging to alter the neural connections associated with these experiences, it's not impossible. The neural connections that you form later in your life are comparatively less rigid than those formed when you were a child, and can be changed more easily. Just as a computer can be reprogrammed with a software upgrade, your mind can be reprogrammed. One effective way to do so is by shifting your perspective and unleashing your inner power.

Consider that everything that happens in your life is for a reason. That reason can stem from a *"victim"* perspective or from a *"creator"* perspective. In the victim perspective these events become limiting beliefs in your program. When there is love, you shift to the creator perspective. These events become learning opportunities—lessons in the game of life which open you up to your highest potential.

Limiting Beliefs and Past Experiences Exercise

This Limiting Beliefs and Past Experiences Exercise will guide you to take inventory of your current mindset, your starting point for unleashing your true powers.

Step 1: Limiting Beliefs Assessment - Take a few minutes to make a list of the limiting beliefs you have about yourself. Perhaps you share limiting beliefs I experienced: *I am not worthy; I am not good enough; I need to be perfect and I never am; I'll never have enough money; I'm afraid to step out of my comfort zone; etc.*

Consider the following categories in making your list:

- Look for pervasive thoughts or assumptions that come up repeatedly. Statements such as: This is just how I am; I've always been this way; that's just how the world is; this is what always happens to me.
- You can also think in terms of current challenges you have in your work life. My opinion doesn't count; my supervisor will never listen to me; no one appreciates me; everyone else gets the good jobs; I have no special

strengths; it's impossible to make money doing something you love; my coworkers don't like me.

- Self-worth beliefs: I am a failure; I don't deserve a better life; it's all my parent's fault.
- Consider challenges that you may have in personal relationships. I can't do something my family doesn't want me to do; my relationships just never work out; all of the good ones are taken; no one wants me.
- There can also be limiting beliefs about money and abundance. I never win free things; there is never enough; earning money requires working really hard; rich people are bad people; making lots of money requires sacrificing who you are.

Step 2: Impactful Past Experiences List: Take a few moments to list the significant past experiences you had that shaped who you are now. The past experiences could be "good" experiences or "not good" experiences you have had. Focus on including experiences where there is a strong emotion involved, such as fear, anger, sadness, or enjoyment. In each of these statements, it is helpful to also include the emotion that would have been felt, whether good or bad. These are some examples from my life experience:

- Being wanted when bribed by my Grandpa with tea to come to him
- The beauty and wonder of the changing colors of leaves in the autumn when I grew up in Rhode Island
- The joy of going to the zoo
- The fear and pain of being spanked with the belt or paddle for doing something "wrong"

- The shame and embarrassment of being made fun of at elementary school
- The frustration of having to eat things that I didn't like
- Feeling embarrassed when speaking in front of a group at work
- Not feeling valued at work

When making your list, it might be helpful to consider the following categories:

- Childhood experiences
- Past challenges
- Family, education, and societal interactions
- Reflecting on past mistakes and successes
- Lessons learned from past events.

Step 3. Shift Your Perspective from Victim to Creator: Review the past experiences in Step 2. For those experiences you judge to be "not good," or perhaps you felt as though you were the victim in that experience, see if you can find a way to shift your perspective. Was there learning that occurred from that experience? What are the possibilities to shift this to a "good" experience in some way? Everything that happens, happens for a reason. Is there another reason this experience happened in your life? Imagine the possibilities and write one or more ways in which this experience could have been to your benefit.

For example, not feeling valued at work - the victim would blame the situation on their coworkers or boss; the creator would say the situation is telling them it was time to make a change in some way.

Congratulations! You have created an honest snapshot of your current mindset. You will use these limiting beliefs and past experiences in the next chapter to shift your perspective, to become the creator of your life.

Next Steps

> *"The combination of your thoughts and feelings is your state of being. Change your state of being... and change your reality."*
>
> - Dr. Joe Dispenza

Awareness of the reality your mind is creating for you is a key part of the solution to any challenge you face in life. You can't change your reality if you don't change your thoughts and beliefs, and acknowledge your current and desired state of being. Unless you have shifted your perspective, your current state of mind is a representation of your limiting beliefs and the state of mind created by your past experiences.

While it may very well be your current reality, know that you have the power to change your reality. You have the power to rewrite your story and overcome your limiting beliefs. You don't have to be the same person you were in that past experience. You are reading this book now because you know this to be true. You are ready to take control of your life.

In the next Chapter, you will learn about an approach to shifting your perspective to overcome your limiting beliefs and past experiences, become the loving creator of your life, and realize your highest potential personally and professionally!

Chapter II

The Power Inside - Shifting Your Perspective

> *"Our thoughts are mainly controlled by our subconscious, which is largely formed before the age of six, and you cannot change the subconscious mind by just thinking about it. That's why the power of positive thinking will not work for most people. The subconscious mind is like a tape player. Until you change the tape, it will not change."*
>
> – BRUCE H. LIPTON, PHD

In this quote, Bruce is highlighting the fact that our mind is largely programmed by our external environment before the age of six! Our actions and reactions won't change unless we change the tape, or in other words, rewrite the programming. To do so requires more than thinking about it. You don't build muscle by thinking about it. Building muscle requires repetitive exercise. Similarly, creating new programs in your mind to unleash your true power and potential requires practice.

Have you ever noticed yourself being reactive or triggered by someone or something? Did you have the feeling that your action was beyond your control, driven by habits, patterns, or beliefs from your past?

How quickly and reliably you can unleash your true power and potential depends upon you and your level of commitment to creating a new reality. For example, if your childhood environment emphasized being the victim by blaming your external circumstances for everything that happened in your life, you may unknowingly repeat this pattern.

In the last chapter, you identified your current mindset. You identified the limiting beliefs and past experiences controlling your thoughts. If you have not yet done this, you should take some time to capture whatever comes to mind. Play some relaxing music while you do this to calm the mind. There is *no right or wrong answer*. Only you know what is true for you. If you did create the list, take a few minutes to review it and see if any additional items arise as being important before proceeding. Of course, you can always go back and add additional items at any time. Perhaps the exercises in this chapter will allow you to identify some additional limiting beliefs and past experiences shaping your current reality.

In this chapter, I will share two practical and proven approaches you can use to unlock and ignite the **Power Inside**. The Power Inside you can be used to shift your perspective and mindset from what it currently is to what you desire it to be. For example, from victim to creator or from where you are now into cultivating a mindset of abundance and gratitude. When you make the shift you not only affect your thoughts, you affect your body, resulting in less physical pain and better health.

There are two key elements to shifting your perspective. First, shifting from being externally focused to internally focused, and second, overcoming *Inner Child Wounds* (which can also be referred to as *anchors*), through loving and nurturing your inner child.

Shifting from Being Externally Focused to Internally Focused

When you were a child, you were dependent upon your parents to love and nurture you. Your very survival was dependent upon your external environment. As a result, you naturally became externally focused. Your thoughts and beliefs are the result of the external environment in which you lived. It was not anything you had any control over at that time. That was the reality in which you lived. You were programmed to be externally focused, programmed to give your power away to those whose responsibility it was to care for you. It's time to take your power back!

Can you think of situations in which you gave away your power? It usually doesn't feel good. In some cases, you might even have felt sick.

When you are externally focused, you are giving your power away to whatever it is you are focused on. It could be a person, or it could be a thing. When you are internally focused, you are bringing your power back into your core. You have so much more power than you realize to be the creator of your reality. The shift from being externally to internally focused empowers you to unleash and ignite the power inside that you were always intended to have available to you. I can think of so many situations in which I gave my power away at work or in relationships with other people. I allowed myself to be triggered by the words and actions of others, thereby giving them my power. One example was becoming hurt or angry about a judgment someone made about me in a meeting at work.

When I was researching different approaches to shift to the power inside myself, I discovered this principle was well explained by Dr. Sue Morter, author of *The Energy Codes* (2020). Dr. Sue Morter contends that many people go through their lives focusing on and absorbed in things in their external environment. In other words, things that they have no control over, outside of themselves. You forget that you have the power to control and take charge of the experiences within your own body. You knowingly or unknowingly throw your energy outside of you onto the object of your attention and anchor your energy there instead of inside yourself. When your focus is on all of these objects outside of you, you can never quite relax because you don't feel safe, strong, or complete.

This can happen in both positive or "*good*" situations, as well as in challenging or "*bad*" situations. For example, when you "lose" yourself in a relationship with something or someone, you can lose your power over your reality to the external object of your affection or attention. When you pull your awareness and focus back inside of yourself, on you, you have so much more power available to handle any challenge or obstacle. Furthermore, when you throw all of your attention onto something or someone, it actually pushes them away.

To demonstrate this point, let's go back to the story in Chapter One, in which I shared about my first husband cheating on me. By putting all of my focus on him, I lost my power. I lost who I was by giving too much of myself to him. I was pushing him away without knowing it at the time, because at that moment in time I didn't realize my focus was on his happiness and not my own. I gave him my power and allowed him to devastate me, not realizing that through my own actions

I was pushing him away from me. I unknowingly pushed him into the affairs he was having behind my back. Yes, after our marriage ended, he finally admitted that there was more than one affair. Because he lied to me about the affairs he was having by not admitting to me it was happening, I filed for divorce and we ended our marriage.

Years later, looking back on what happened there was a revelation. I realized the truth was I created the situation through my thoughts and actions. With this realization, I was finally able to take my power back by forgiving myself and forgiving him. I was no longer judging myself as the victim. I shifted my perspective to loving compassion by understanding that I didn't know any better at the time. I willingly and unknowingly gave my power in the relationship away. I wasn't the victim. I was indeed the creator of my reality by being "externally focused" on him and not being "internally focused" on me in our relationship.

Have you ever had to give a presentation in front of a group of strangers and felt nervous? What is that nervousness all about? It's another example of being externally focused. I used to be terrified of speaking in front of strangers. The palms of my hands became wet. My voice became shaky. Instead of focusing on breathing deeply into my core and being confident, I was focused on how they would judge me. I was worried they wouldn't like me, or might question my credibility, or ask me a question I didn't know how to answer. I was throwing my power out to my audience. I was externally focused. There really wasn't any need to be nervous, if only I had been internally focused.

When I shift my focus or perspective to the inside of me instead of my external environment, it no longer matters to me what other people think about me. It no longer matters how others may or may not "judge" me, because I have taken back control, taken back my power over my thoughts. I am fully responsible for my feelings. I am able to express myself with confidence, grace and ease.

Shifting your focus from outside of yourself to inside of yourself—from external to internal—makes all the difference in the results you get in relationships, at work, and in creative endeavors. You become less conditional and less dependent on the outer world because you have taken back control of your inner power and freedom to express your magnificence.

Practice: Shifting from Externally Focused to Internally Focused

The intention of this practice is to increase your awareness of how you feel when you are focused on your external environment versus internally, on the self. It is called a practice because it will take repetition (practice as many times as needed in different situations) to change your programming from defaulting to external focus, training (or reprogramming) you to default to internal focus. Once you can feel the difference in the body, you will become better at shifting and maintaining your focus on yourself (internally) in everyday situations. This is your position of Power Inside. This is from where you are the creator of your reality. You can refer to the Figure below for this exercise.

Step 1 - *Identify an object to use for the practice.*

Imagine someone just walked into the room and is standing at the door, calling your attention to them. You can also place your attention on an object or pet that is in the room or outside a window. Anything will work for this exercise.

Step 2 - *Place all of your focus and attention on the external object you identified.*

Really concentrate on the object. Imagine feeling as if you are throwing all of your energy into the outside of your body onto the object you are focusing on. You can even focus on the object with love if it helps to imagine it more fully.

Step 3 - *Pull your focus and attention back into yourself.*

You are calling your attention back to you, inside of your body. Imagine feeling that you are inside your body looking out through your own eyes.

Step 4 – *Observe and notice how you feel.*

What were the sensations or feelings you experienced when you shifted your attention back inside your body after being focused externally on an object? If you didn't catch it the first time, try it again. Just like muscles need to be trained, you are training yourself to notice how different it feels to be externally versus internally focused. You may have the sensation of being back home, being back in your body again. You may feel contracted when you are sending all of your energy outside of you and expanded when you bring all of your energy back inside your body. Write down the differences you are feeling.

Step 5 – *Breathe deeply.*

Take several deep belly breaths in and out while holding the awareness of focusing inside your body.

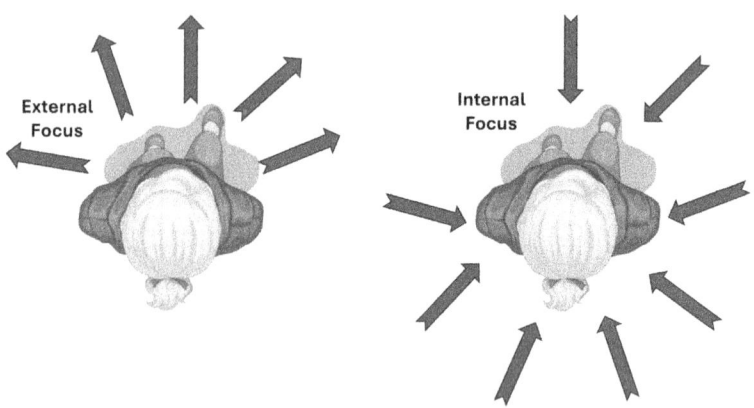

Internal-External-Internal Exercise

Now that you know what it means to shift from being externally to internally focused, you can better connect with and overcome your inner child wounds.

Overcoming Inner Child Wounds

In Chapter One, you created a list of limiting beliefs and past experiences. When your needs aren't met as a child, those memories and experiences can stick around and resurface long into your adulthood. Who you have become as an adult is directly informed by your childhood experiences. Can you recall a childhood memory in which you had a particularly good or bad experience? Perhaps you felt misunderstood, ignored, or afraid. For example, when I was a child my Dad would pretend he was throwing me in the pool to teach me how to swim. I was unable to be submerged in water until I was a year old due to a rare birthmark on my spine. I was terrified! This created an inner child wound associated with fear.

No matter what you have faced in the past, you likely have an inner child that needs to be taken care of, especially if you have had past experiences that you haven't healed from or fully processed. These needs, or *Inner Child Wounds*, manifest themselves in your life as limiting beliefs.

Inner Child Wounds are the unhealed parts of ourselves formed in response to unmet needs or painful experiences from early childhood. These situations most likely occurred before the age of nine and are often associated with not feeling safe, loved, or not receiving needed attention from your parents. They can also result from bad experiences at school, such as being yelled at by a teacher or feeling rejected by playmates. People with inner child wounds may suffer from low self-esteem, have difficulty trusting others, or struggle to express their emotions.

You can overcome your Inner Child Wounds through loving and nurturing your inner child. Think about a time in your life or recently when you were reactive. Being reactive means that you are allowing someone else to take your power. It means that you are not taking full responsibility for your actions and feelings. You are acting in response to a situation or person rather than creating the reality you desire from the inside out. When you are being reactive, the truth is that your inner child is throwing a temper tantrum. Yes, a temper tantrum! These are aspects of you that never grew up. They react to anything that isn't in alignment with what they want or think.

The reactive aspect or aspects of your inner child are essentially holding you back from being the best you can be. A few common examples of how inner child wounds can manifest in your life: low self-esteem or self worth—blaming yourself when things go wrong, or being overly harsh or critical of yourself; emotional repression—not allowing yourself to feel or express emotions; not being able to express your wants or needs—instead letting others make all of the decisions for you, which may or may not be in your highest good; distrust—not being able to trust others in relationships

Unless you have done the inner child work or grew up in a perfect, nurturing, and loving environment, your inner child can be triggered and become reactive, giving away your power. You can also think of reactivity as your "triggers." Triggers are often related to past experiences that create an emotional response or reaction. Can you think of some situations in which you became triggered?

When I first started on my journey to become the creator of my life, I had many aspects of my inner child self that were reactive. When I actually started paying attention to what I was reacting to, I couldn't believe how many aspects of myself needed love and nurturing. While I thought I was pretty good at "controlling them," the truth is that they were controlling me! There were times when they would just take over my mind and actions. They were always present in my mind, letting me know when they were unhappy.

For instance, the "Not Good Enough" aspect of me would always freak out when I needed to speak up in a meeting or give a presentation at work. "Dad told us to be quiet or we would get in big trouble!" My palms would become sweaty and cold no matter how much I told her that it was safe to speak, that we didn't need to be quiet anymore. My face would turn red with shame for speaking up. The "Not Good Enough" aspect didn't feel "good enough" to be listened to. She lacked confidence in speaking up, in speaking her truth.

She was always present when I was in a meeting with my superiors at work. In fact, that was what held me back from my last promotion. I'll never forget that day. I was given the opportunity to interview for the Director of Advanced Satellite

Programs position. I really wanted to be selected to lead the organization and take the next step in my career and in creating the future. The interview panel consisted of four men. They asked me questions that I was prepared to answer, but the words didn't—couldn't—come out. The "Not Good Enough" aspect of me was too afraid to speak up and share my ideas. I wasn't good enough to express myself with confidence. One of the interviewers told me after the interview that he was surprised my answers were so poor because he knew I had great ideas. It cost me that promotion and the opportunity to be considered for other promotions.

For many years I thought I was doing great and living at my highest potential, telling myself, "I am happy." Then I realized that I couldn't even answer a simple question: How are you feeling today? What a simple question, right? My response was always quick and noncommittal. "I'm good thank you!" "I'm fine, thank you!" Truth is, I didn't really know how I felt, because I was suppressing most of my emotions. I buried all of the emotions I didn't want to feel. Emotions I didn't want to feel because it was painful to feel them due to something that had happened when I was a child. I buried them because I didn't want to be hurt. As a result, I couldn't feel anything. You might say I had become "Comfortably Numb," just like the Pink Floyd song!

I have been working on feeling that which had been locked away inside of me, working on releasing and nurturing the aspects of myself that I locked up and abandoned many years ago. Yes, it takes time, patience, and love. Yes, there are many, many, many tears, which sometimes come with trembling and shaking. It's just like working with an unhappy child.

Everything happens for a reason, and it is good even if we don't know the reason at the moment. Inner child wounds heal by loving them deeply, loving them compassionately with consistent nurturing, reinforcing positive behaviors, and helping them to clearly understand that all is good now and they are safe. Letting them know that you will never abandon them again, you will always be there for them. Letting them know that they have a voice again. They are loved, cherished, protected, and home in your heart!

There are **common inner child wounds** many people develop in childhood, mostly between birth and the age of six. These are some examples and how they may manifest and could be addressed in your life:

Rejection (or Ignored) – When you feel rejected or ignored. When you feel as if you are not included, approved of, or accepted. Being rejected or ignored can make you feel unwanted and not good enough. It can lead to you putting up emotional walls around your heart as I did when my husband cheated on me, or when my Dad told me I couldn't speak until spoken to. This can also result from being bullied as a child on the schoolyard or being the last one selected for a team in Physical Education.

Since the Rejected One feels rejected, this inner child wound can also manifest as wanting to reject things in your life. It can show up as denying yourself what you want by making it appear to others that you don't care, when you really do care, usually more than you will admit to yourself. You tell yourself that other people don't really understand you, so why let them into your heart just to end up feeling rejected by them? You never give yourself a chance to truly succeed or be loved.

Ask the rejected one inside what it would take to not feel rejected or ignored? Explore how it might be possible to shift your perspective about the situation.

Abandonment – Abandonment issues can arise from life events such as losing a loved one, experiencing divorce or separation, feeling betrayed in a relationship, facing chronic illness, enduring parental separation, being adopted or in foster care, or suffering abuse. All of these life events can result in feelings of abandonment.

An abandonment wound is a deep emotional feeling of being left behind, unloved, or unimportant. This wound can manifest in various ways in adulthood, such as low self-esteem, difficulty trusting others, depression and feelings of worthlessness, challenges with effective communication, and difficulties with intimacy. It often leads to difficulties in forming stable, trusting relationships.

Let the abandoned one know that you are there for them and will never abandon them again. Ask them what they need from you for them to not feel abandoned.

Not good enough or not worthy – perhaps this is something that one or more of your parents or siblings instilled in you through their words or actions. Like rejection, this feeling can be generated in the school environment through school work, such as not getting good enough grades, or even on the playground with other kids (not being physically or emotionally able to compete effectively, not getting picked to be on a team); you tried your best and you still weren't as good as you wanted to be.

Sometimes you can feel like you're not good enough because you're comparing yourself to others who are in different circumstances. You may also be comparing your own weaknesses to another person's strengths. It's important to remember that everyone has their own unique journey.

Realize that being good enough or not good enough is subjective. It's not a fact. It's not black and white. It is relative, a judgment. If something is not good enough, the question to ask your inner child is what would it take to make it good enough? Be curious about how you can shift your inner child's perspective about what is good enough.

Impatient – you probably experienced situations where you wanted something to happen as soon as possible. You might have been unwilling to wait for something and consequently became unhappy or annoyed because it didn't happen when you wanted it to. No doubt every one of you had many times when you were impatient as a child. Impatient for attention. Impatient for food. Impatient to go outside and play. Impatient for a reward.

Perhaps what you are being impatient about is beyond your control. Consider that it may be in your highest good to be patient in that 'now' moment. What would it require to shift the Impatient one's perspective to being patient?

Perfectionist – you may have had early life experiences in which you felt your worth was conditional upon meeting certain standards or expectations. This could have been imposed by parents, caregivers, teachers, or society. These types of experiences might result in internalizing the belief that you must be flawless to be loved, valued, or accepted. Over time, this mindset can solidify into perfectionism. Perhaps you felt that you needed to excel in every aspect of your life to gain approval from those you loved. You may have developed a fear of failure to avoid rejection or disapproval, resulting in feeling that you needed to always be perfect.

Feelings of unworthiness, shame, and a deep sense of inadequacy may manifest as chronic stress, burnout, and strained relationships. Relationships are strained in many cases due to feeling the need to criticize others. Perfectionism interferes with your ability to relax, connect with others, and enjoy life by embracing imperfections. It also often results in self-criticism and harsh judgment of self and others.

When you observe yourself stressing about being perfect or making something perfect, ask your inner perfectionist to reframe the situation: What would it take to be as good as possible? What would have to be true for something or someone to be perfect enough to be perceived as perfect? Are you setting unrealistically high expectations? Are you quick to find fault? Are you overly critical of what you view as mistakes? Are you trying to avoid failure or harsh judgment?

One thing you might have noticed is that most of these wounds are based upon an *external* focus. Yes, there are things in your outer world that are causing these things to be *triggers*. They are the result of not taking responsibility for your feelings. Even so, some of these triggers will only be shifted when the one that is being reactive is loved and nurtured. A baby doesn't just stop crying on its own. The baby must be loved and made to feel safe.

Using your list of limiting beliefs and past experiences, take a few moments now to add to each item the Inner Child Wounds. Add to the list any specific triggers and the Inner Child aspect of yourself that is most likely responsible. You can start with the list of examples I provided above if they feel relevant for you. There can certainly be others as well, such as: not respected, overwhelmed, fear of not having enough (money, time, other), worrier, avoiding confrontation, not trusting, controlling, sad, scared, unsafe, disappointed, angry, judging, or blaming. Which ones resonate with you?

Think about situations in which you felt *triggered* by something or someone in your external environment. What were you feeling? What was the emotion that arose in you? It is most likely an Inner Child wound. It is most likely your Inner

Child being reactive to your external environment. What do you do? How do you shift your perspective?

As Dr. Wayne W. Dyer, a renowned author and speaker on self-development and spiritual growth once said: *"You cannot always control what goes on outside. But you can always control what goes on inside."* That's the **Power Inside**!

These are examples of how you can nurture or heal your inner child by shifting your perspective:

There was a time when I would be very impatient and annoyed with slow drivers. The ***Impatient One*** inside me would become reactive, saying, "Why can't this idiot drive? I wish they would get over into the slow lane? Please move!!" If I could, I would speed up and go around them. If I couldn't get around them, I would just feel my blood pressure rising as I became more annoyed. Once I realized I was being reactive, I asked, "Who is being reactive now?" As you might imagine, it was the Impatient One and the Annoyed One. The Impatient One was an inner child wound created around the time I was a year old. My Mom wouldn't take me out of my crib when I called her. It was devastating because I wanted to be able to see what was going on, to be free.

After following the steps I will share shortly, I created a shift. Now I play a "game" with these aspects of myself, which also has the added benefit of shifting my focus to my internal environment. I told the Impatient and Annoyed One that whenever this happens, we will play a game of "being patient and calm." I explained to them, lovingly, we win the game if we can be patient when we start to feel impatient. We win the game if we remain calm and happy when something is annoying us. I shifted their perspectives and consequently changed the outcome of the triggering situation. Yes, it did take more than one conversation! But then, it was a really deep wound.

One more example to clarify the process. This one is about the **Perfectionist**. I have a tendency to desire to have everything be "perfect." Whenever I would give a presentation at work, I wanted it to be perfect. Perfect words, perfect slides, perfect everything. I would set such high expectations for myself that it was impossible to be perfect enough for my inner perfectionist. She would always criticize and judge me, telling me what I didn't do perfectly enough for her.

Again, it's about shifting your perspective. It's about helping your reactive inner child to shift their perspective. Isn't that what you do with a child that is having a temper tantrum? Patiently and lovingly working with the **Perfectionist** inside of me, I have been able to shift her perspective. I have forgiven and embraced this aspect of myself. Now after I give a speech, she has learned to say that it was perfect at that moment. She no longer criticizes or judges me for what I did or didn't do, said or didn't say.

The power is in shifting your inner child's perspective or focus from what they can't have, driven by the external world, to what they can have, *created* by the internal world—the **Power Inside**. Be curious about what is really needed to make something perfect "enough"? If it is unobtainable or an unrealistic expectation, then it can never be achieved, and it will never be "perfect." However, it can be perfect when you shift your perspective. By working with my inner perfectionist, I have learned how to accept things as perfect enough, eliminating the reactive perfectionist inside of me. I no longer have a tendency to be critical of others which haqs significantly improved the quality of my relationships.

Overcoming Inner Child Wounds Exercise

Healing your inner child is a journey that requires patience, self-compassion, and persistence. It's about embracing all of you, all of your imperfections and recognizing that you are enough just as you are now. By addressing the root causes of your wounds and nurturing your inner child, you can create a more balanced, fulfilling, and joyful life. It only takes three simple steps to shift your Inner Child's perspective.

Step 1: Be the observer.

When you observe that you are being reactive or triggered, ask yourself this question: "Who is being triggered? Which aspect of my inner child is feeling the need to be reactive?" In some cases, there can be more than one aspect that is being reactive. No doubt you have seen siblings trigger one another to be reactive. Start with the one that feels the most reactive. I have found that in many cases, shifting the perspective of the most triggered aspect helps all of the triggered aspects.

By being the observer and focusing your attention inside of you, on your inner child, you are giving your inner child something that they need. They are being reactive because they have a need that isn't being met in some way causing them and consequently you to feel triggered. When you give them a voice by asking them what they need, they feel valued. To truly heal, you need to embrace and acknowledge every aspect of your inner child.

Step 2: Love each and every one inside of you that is being triggered.

Love is the answer. There are no problems, only solutions. First, tell the triggered one that you love them and forgive them. Be patient and compassionate with your words and assure them you are there to help them feel better. Remember every aspect of yourself is a precious part of yourself that deserves to feel loved and safe. If you're not sure, ask them what they are being reactive about. Then, ask them what they need to stop being reactive. Address their specific concerns just as you would do with a child having a temper tantrum. Help the inner child to reframe the perceived challenges, setbacks, or obstacles into opportunities. Help them to shift their perspective and realize that they do have what they need. They have your attention and love. Reassure them that you are always there for them, loving them no matter what.

You may need to explain to each triggered aspect of your Inner Child that all is good. Speak to them as if you were speaking to the child version of yourself. Imagine that you are able to travel back in time and comfort your younger self. Let them know that everything is okay. Most of your inner child wounds are the result of you not feeling safe, loved, or recognized as a child. You may also have experienced physical or emotional trauma resulting in fear. To heal, they need to know you will be there for them. Help them to understand that you will make sure they feel safe, protected and loved. There is no longer any need for them to be afraid or reactive.

Step 3: Shift your focus from the external to the inner world.

Shift your focus from things you have no control over in your external environment to what you can control in your internal environment—your Inner Child's reactions. Shift your focus to taking responsibility for what you are feeling instead of blaming or judging something or someone in your external environment. Observe your thoughts and feelings. Don't let your inner child control you. If the 'monkey mind' is talking to you, ask who it is that is unhappy, who is being reactive. Which aspect of you needs help? Then love them as described in Step 2. Repeat as needed!

When you shift your focus to your internal environment, your inner child feels more valued and nurtured, helping them to heal what happened in the past.

Step 4: Use this approach for known areas of reactivity.

If you know that certain aspects of yourself tend to become reactive, you can follow Step 2 and 3 in a proactive manner. Speak with them lovingly to let them know that you support and love them. Ask them to tell you what they need to feel loved and safe.

As a practical tool, I have found that taking time to connect with my inner child on a daily basis and capture the conversation in a personal journal is very helpful. If possible, connect and check-in with your inner child to identify any aspects that may be feeling triggered about something that happened in the past, or in anticipation of something that will happen in the future. Take time to speak to them and help them overcome their reactivity.

Step 5. Create an action plan

Take a few moments now to write down some specific actions you will take to shift your perspective the next time you feel yourself being reactive or triggered. What actions, if any, do you intend to take daily to contribute to the healing of your inner child? I provided a suggestion in Step 4 based upon my personal experience. The key is to find a plan you can commit to, so that you can take back control of your destiny.

Next Steps

> *"With everything that has happened to you, you can either feel sorry for yourself or treat what has happened as a gift. Everything is either an opportunity to grow or an obstacle to keep you from growing. You get to choose."*
>
> ~ WAYNE DYER

This quote by Wayne Dyer is a perfect example of what it means to shift your perspective. Another way to look at this is that everything that has happened or will happen in your life has happened for a reason. You get to choose the reason. You have the **Power Inside** of you to decide if it is a learning opportunity for you or an obstacle to keep you from making your dreams a reality and creating a life you love living.

Congratulations! You are fully ready to harness your **Power Inside** as a creator of your life. Now you know the feelings associated with being internally focused versus externally focused, and have a practical tool you can use to continue to strengthen your ability to shift your focus inside. You can take back your power. You also have a better understanding of how your inner child wounds might be holding you back from your highest potential, and how to approach healing them for a more fulfilled life. With this foundation, we will next explore how to set intentions and goals aligned with your new mindset.

Chapter III

The Power of Intention - Setting Intentions for What You Truly Desire

> *"When you're clear on your intention, you take inspired action that's in alignment with your words and truth. You also quickly manifest what you desire because you're clearly putting out words and actions that are in alignment with the things you want to attract into your life."*
>
> ~ STEPHENIE ZAMORA
> (CREATOR OF "THE FUTURE OF LIFE PURPOSE DEVELOPMENT")

Stephanie Zamora's quote rings true for me, not only from my experience, but also from the standpoint of my scientific background. According to quantum science, everything in the universe, from the trees to the air you breathe, and the people you love, is composed of energy. Quantum physicists have shown that energy can be both a particle and a wave. A particle is still, a wave is in motion. In quantum physics, the observer principle suggests that particles exist in a state of probability (or infinite possibility) until they are observed. Once observed the particles collapse into a definite state. In other words, they collapse into a specific reality.

Based upon quantum physics experiments it has been shown that the mind can influence the state of the physical world, your reality. Specifically, that the intentions, emotions, and desires of an experimenter may influence experimental outcomes, even in controlled and blinded experimental designs. Since thoughts and intentions are also forms of energy, they interact with and influence the physical world around us. In other words, intention acts as a guiding energy, shaping actions and outcomes in your life. When your intention is clear, it becomes easier to recognize and take aligned, inspired action, allowing you to move forward with greater grace and ease.

When setting intentions, it is important to focus your attention internally as you practiced in the last chapter. You want the focus of your intentions to be on what you need to create from your internal world, not driven by the people and situations around you. If you sense any reactivity from your Inner Child, you know how you can shift your Inner Child's perspective by being loving, nurturing, and supportive when speaking with them. You have shifted your perspective from being a victim to being the creator, based upon the **Power Inside**. The powers that have always been inside of you are waiting to be unleashed.

It's time to tap into what you truly desire inside your heart of hearts by using the **Power of Intention.** Time for you to set your intentions or vision for what you want to create in your life from the inside out. Since you are no longer the victim of your external world, what do you want to create in your life? You and only you are responsible. You have the power to blossom and create the life of your dreams. A key element of this process is commitment. Specifically, making a commitment to what you desire to create in your life by writing it down. You can write it with a pen and paper, or you can type it into a document on your computer, whichever works best for you. Studies show that you are 42 percent more likely to accomplish your goals if you take the time to write them down.

Goals are specific, measurable objectives that provide direction and structure to your actions. They represent the results you aim to achieve based on your thought process. Goals focus on external accomplishments. Did you catch that word I just used? *External.* What's that about? Goals are tangible and can be clearly checked off a list based upon an "external" observation. For example, a goal might be "Go to Hawaii," or "Learn to make cheesecake." When setting a goal, the emphasis is placed on both the result and the journey along the way. You track milestones and assess progress toward the objective. Yes, goals are externally focused.

Intentions are the underlying purpose and motivation behind your actions. They are more about the "energy" you put in at the very start of something. Intentions focus on your relationship with yourself. An intention describes how you want to feel "internally." For instance, an intention could be to feel joyful, abundant, grateful, or peaceful. Intentions allow you to create alignment in your life. They serve as a chosen theme, a comprehensive purpose, or an attitude you commit to. Intentions guide your actions and shape the fabric of your experiences. Intentions are more about the feelings you want to create inside.

Setting up intentions for your vision can do magic for your motivation, persistence, and your overall satisfaction in the process of achieving your goals. Intentions make your mind more focused. Intentions make your mind think about your body and soul, your life purpose and desires. Recall in the last chapter where you learned about internal versus external focus. When you are focused internally, you are focused on the feelings and emotions you are creating on the inside. You are creating your external reality from the inside out, based upon the feelings you intend to create. What do you want to feel? Love? Happiness? Joy? Gratitude? Abundance? Setting intentions might be the secret weapon that you're missing, especially if you struggle with staying on track and fulfilling your goals.

With many of the courses I have taken on my journey, a common theme around intention is this: when your intention and behavior match, when your actions and thoughts are the same, when your mind and body are working together, when your words and your truth are in alignment, you unleash an immense and magnificent power within to be the creator of your life. Yes! Everyone of us is born with this power inside of us. It's up to you to find the desire and courage to unlock this power and manifest your true destiny.

When I was a child, my family lived in constant fear of not having enough money. My Mom and Dad did the best they could. My Dad worked two jobs. My Mom worked third shift so she could be at home with the kids during the day. There wasn't a lot of time for fun or joy. I realized at a very young age that I didn't want to, and I wouldn't, live my life like that, if at all possible. I set an intention to obtain a college degree in a field where I wouldn't need to worry about having enough money.

My first real job was when I attended high school. I had been awarded the opportunity to travel to Washington, DC to attend the Presidential Classroom for Young Americans. My parents didn't have the money to pay for the airfare and hotel. They told me I had to get a job if I really wanted to go. I found a job at McDonalds. Talk about motivation to get an education and a better paying job. While there were some fun times, working with the public clearly demonstrated to me that I did not want to make McDonald's my career job!

My intention was to get a degree in *"something."* Something that didn't involve working with the public every day. Being one of the best students in my high school math and physics classes, I decided to attend UCLA for an engineering degree. I left home and moved in with my boyfriend as soon as I turned 18. My Dad wasn't happy. He told me I would get pregnant and drop out of college. He bet me $300 I would never finish college, further fueling my motivation and intention to graduate from UCLA and become an engineer. This intention to live a better life than what I was born into shaped my choices and gave me the determination to pursue a life beyond my family's struggles. Of course, he gave me the $300 when I graduated and secured an entry level engineering position working on satellite systems.

Intentions are powerful tools for creating your reality. Creating intentions has worked for me, and I believe it can also work for you. The reality is that I never would have graduated from college if I hadn't intended for it to be so. It was what I truly wanted to do, what I wanted to create in my life. It wasn't my parents telling me that was what I needed to do. My goal was to create a life in which I didn't need to be worried about having enough money every day, as I'd seen my parents do. To achieve that goal, I set an intention to obtain a college degree. I felt that with a college degree I could get a better paying job, be happier, and feel more secure and safe. I would be in a position to help my parents as they became older and could no longer work. Because I established this goal for myself, my parents and I no longer need to fear having enough money to live with the basic necessities of life.

You can also use intentions in the work environment. I often used intentions with my technology development teams when we were developing a proposal for one of my customers. This was really effective when it was a competitive proposal that we really wanted to win. There were a couple of nuances in making the intention effective. First, the intention needed to be in alignment with the highest value evaluation criteria for the proposal. In other words, what was the most important selection criteria for the customer? Second, there had to be alignment amongst the team members with the intention for our offering or proposed solution. If anyone on the team had a conflicting intention, it would impact the ability of the team to create the best solution and winning proposal for the customer.

Another example of how I used setting intentions in work situations was making professional interactions more purposeful and aligned with my goals. At some point in my career, following the advice from my Executive Coach, I set the intention to sit next to specific superiors or potential customers during important business meetings. By setting intentions to connect with key executives with an explicit purpose for what I desired to achieve with that engagement, I found that my focus led to more impactful and positive conversations and outcomes.

When you start the journey toward your vision for your life, you won't know every step that will be required on your journey. You set an intention for your first step. Once that step is completed, the path forward will become more clear, in divine, right timing. Trust that you will know what is needed next, what that next intention will be when you get there. It may be hard to believe, but you will discover that is the truth. This is the truth I have experienced.

Even if you take a step in a direction that is not aligned with your vision, you will realize that you need to course correct. Your intuitive inner voice, which I talk about in Chapter VII, will guide you on your journey when you learn how to listen to that voice. The truth is there are infinite possibilities. There are an infinite number of ways to get from where you are now to achieving your vision. There is never a right or wrong answer. Every step you take is part of your unique journey in the game of life. Every step is "perfect" for you!

Setting Intentions Exercise

In this exercise you will think about what you really desire. It is important to create intentions for what you really desire for yourself, not what you think others want for you. It must be heartfelt; it needs to come from inside of you. It's not about what other people may have or may say, it is about what you really desire. It's about the desires that are perfect for you now, in the present moment. Create your intentions in a statement, as if they have already happened. You have the freedom to create a life of abundance, love and joy!

Here are some examples of intention statements you can create for yourself:

- I am a college graduate. I love being a college graduate in electrical engineering.
- I love creating the future.
- I love exploring infinite possibilities.

- I am the creator of my dream life.
- I am the perfect weight.
- I have a healthy spine and bones.
- I am abundant! I am vitality!
- I ignite my power as creator.
- I allow myself to blossom into my magnificence.

It's all up to you! There are infinite possibilities for you to create. For example, the first time I did this for myself I had single word intentions: Abundance, Vitality, Passion, and Happiness. Even though many years have passed, I still carry these words with me on a piece of paper.

Now you're ready to take some time to write down your goals and intentions on a piece of paper. Or you can type them into a document on your computer or phone.

Step 1: Write down the feelings you desire to have in your life.

Identify the feelings you want to cultivate in your life, like love, joy, or abundance. Which feelings are important to you now?

Step 2: Write down intentions that could result in creating those feelings.

Be curious about the possibilities to create these feelings in your life. Remember, there are infinite possibilities! It's more important for you to have intentions about how you want to feel than a goal. The goals needed to achieve the intention will emerge step by step. For example, I am spending more time meditating to create more peace in my life; I am expressing gratitude every day for my blessings to create more abundance.

Step 3: Select the top three intentions for which you feel the strongest alignment or resonance.

To help you stay more focused and aligned with these top three, write them down on sticky notes or a piece of paper. Place the intentions you wrote down someplace where you will see them every day. It can be as simple as a one-word intention, or it can be a statement similar to the ones I shared at the beginning of this section. For example, by setting intentions to connect with key executives, I found that my focus led to more impactful and positive conversations.

Step 4: Maintain alignment of your actions with your intentions.

Before you take action or make a decision, ask yourself, "Will this generate the feelings that I created in my intention? Is this creating the feelings that I intended to create?" To maintain alignment with your goals and intentions, review them on a regular basis. This can be done daily, weekly, monthly, or whenever you need to make an important decision. I review my intentions daily, specifically every morning before I start reading emails, to ensure all my actions during the day are in alignment. I highly recommend that you adopt that approach. It's important to find a time and frequency that works best for you, and that you can commit to. Revise them if needed to make them clearer and more aligned.

Step 5: Celebrate your successes!

It helps to acknowledge the significant steps that you accomplish toward achieving your goals and intentions. By doing so, you reinforce your belief in your ability to be the creator of your life. Keep track of your wins. You got this!

If you're not really sure what you desire, you can create a "Vision Board" to help you manifest your desires and set your intentions. Observe the feelings and emotions that arise when you look at the images on your vision board. A vision board is a collage of images that represent your goals, intentions, and feelings. You can create one by gathering images from magazines, or your photo libraries, and arranging them on a board.

Here are a couple of vision board resources you can use if needed:

1. This *Psychology Today* article offers a simple approach to a Vision Board based upon content from The Berkeley Well-Being Institute: "What Is a Vision Board and Why Make One?" It provides a different perspective on the topic with suggestions for focus areas. Link to article: https://www.psychologytoday.com/us/blog/click-here-happiness/202103/what-is-vision-board-and-why-make-one

2. This article from Oprah Winfrey's Oprah Daily Website is more recent, and provides a nice image of what a Vision Board actually looks like once completed: "How to Make a Vision Board That Actually Works." The article also provides more motivational points associated with creating a Vision Board. Link to article: https://www.oprahdaily.com/life/a29959841/how-to-make-a-vision-board/

Next Steps

"You get what you intend to create by being in harmony with the power of intention, which is responsible for all of creation."

~ WAYNE DYER

This quote by Wayne Dyer about the **Power of Intention** highlights the key point in this Chapter: you have the power to be the creator of your life! By harnessing the energy of your intentions, you gain the ability to effortlessly attract the people, circumstances, and opportunities necessary for your personal growth and fulfillment. The power to manifest your dreams and aspirations lies within you, waiting to be unleashed through the cultivation of intention.

If you are curious about the **Power of Intention** and would like to explore this power more deeply, there is a wonderful book written by Wayne Dyer called *The Power of Intention: Learning to Co-create Your World Your Way*. In this insightful work, Wayne Dyer explores the profound impact that intention can have on your life, and emphasizes the importance of aligning your thoughts, beliefs, and actions with your deepest desires and highest values. The primary theme of the book revolves around the idea that intention is a creative force that shapes your reality.

Congratulations! If you completed the exercise, you now have goals and intentions to chart your course to being the best you and creating a life of love, joy and abundance. Now it's time to take inspired action on making your goals and intentions a reality. You are off to a great start! Through the **Power Inside** you and the **Power of Intention**, you have identified what is important to you. In the next chapter, you will learn about taking inspired actions to create your intended reality.

Chapter IV

Power of Inspired Action

"Take the first step in faith. You don't have to see the whole staircase, just take the first step."

~ Dr. Martin Luther King Jr.

I love this quote by Martin Luther King Jr. For many of you, it may be that first step that is the most difficult to take. It often requires trust and courage. In some cases you may need to overcome fear. You may not know all the answers when you start the journey. You have to trust that you will know what to do when it is time to take that next step. Inspired action is that next step you feel drawn to take, fueled by your excitement and sense of purpose. Have you ever felt that pull toward something, even if you weren't sure where it would lead?

You charted a course to your innermost desires, goals, and intentions in the last chapter. As you continue on your journey to become the creator of your life with the new version of you that is based upon the **Power Inside**, it's time to take inspired action. As you did when establishing your intentions, it is important to take action from the inside out. You are creating a life you love living, in which you love yourself. As Tony Robbins said: "The only impossible journey is the one you never begin."

As a child, watching *Star Trek* sparked my interest in space. "To boldly go where no one has gone before!" Traveling to faraway places, meeting people or beings from other planets, and being transported from one place to another seemingly magically excited me and ignited my imagination. From that seed, I ultimately pursued a degree in engineering, each step motivated by my desire to create the future.

I knew when I was in high school that I would attend college. Coming from a poor background and being the first one in my family to go to college, I had no idea what field to pursue. Then one day, my High School Physics teacher told me about an event taking place at UCLA, sponsored by the Society of Women Engineers for girls in high school. As I said in the last chapter, the aligned path magically emerges! Listening to my inner voice—or intuition—I was inspired to take action, and attended the event. The first step in my aligned path.

I learned that being an engineer involved using math and science skills to create the future. I learned that it was engineers who created the ability to fly to the moon. Wow! How cool was that for a high school girl who always loved science fiction and *Star Trek*? I felt so excited and inspired that I decided that day to take the necessary actions to become an engineer.

I was inspired next to choose UCLA's Bachelor of Science in Engineering program, which provided experience in all engineering disciplines. I didn't need to decide the next step, which discipline, until after the second year when I had been exposed to the different possibilities. Perfect! After understanding the paths available to me, I was most passionate about being a system engineer, working across all of those disciplines. Something deep inside of me said, "*Yes, that is the best choice!*"

Four years later, when I graduated, I had multiple job offers. In the end, the action that inspired me, spoke to my heart, and made me feel the most excited was taking a position working at Hughes Space and Communications where I could—guess what?—work on creating the future with space technology! My **Power of Inspired Action** led me to my dream job!

Since I was working in a job aligned with my passion for creating the future, I excelled at what I was doing. I became known as the technology developer "Secret Weapon," due to my ability to lead teams and grow externally funded contracts from nothing to over $60M. Step by inspired step, promotion by promotion, I achieved happiness and success. I remember feeling both excited and a little afraid when I was offered the opportunity to be promoted to an Executive level as the Director of Advanced Technology Development. This was an enterprise level role reporting to the Vice President and requiring a different set of skills.

I was really stepping out of my comfort zone and was grateful for the recognition. In this role, I was responsible for a research portfolio of $100M! I loved being responsible for making internal investment decisions and finding ways to leverage external development funds. I listened to my intuition, my gut, and I created a fun and collaborative work environment by leading from my heart.

As you can see, I was initially inspired by a TV show to imagine the possibility of working on space technologies and creating the future. I had no idea what was involved or how I would make it happen, but the seed was planted. That seed inspired the actions that I would take in divine right timing. The only way for me to make that a reality was to break out of the environmental programming I grew up in and be the first person to graduate from college in my family. By aligning my decisions and actions with this inspirational seed, I was able to achieve my desire, my dream in life of not being worried about having enough money. Step by step, action by inspired action, I achieved my vision, my dream. You can do it too, through the **Power of Inspired Action**!

What early dreams did you have? Do you recall any actions you have taken that you felt excited or passionate about?

What is an inspired action?

Inspired action is when you feel a deep-rooted passion and motivation to do something. It's a feeling inside of you. A feeling means that you are tapping into your emotions. There is an emotional response. It could be feeling joy when you think about the result of taking that action. It could be a feeling of expansion, bliss, or a tingling sensation all over your body. Maybe it's just a feeling inside your gut or a voice inside your head that says, "*Yes, that is the right path now, in the present moment.*" Think about a time when you felt motivated or passionate about doing something. What did you feel?

Inspired action is simple, fluid, and exciting. It's focused on what you truly desire. When you take action guided by inspiration, you feel capable and excited. Your dream overshadows your fear, and there's no sacrifice, just dedication. There is no fear or worry that you are making the wrong decision, choosing the wrong path. There is only joy, grace, and ease, because you chose the path that is in alignment with your true desires, your heart's desires, and your dreams.

You are truly inspired to make it so! You have most likely taken inspired actions in your life. Most people do so without even realizing that is what they are doing. Perhaps you had a strong inner urge to take action. Maybe it was a gut feeling or intuition. There might have been powerful emotions (mostly positive) associated with the idea or action. You may not have known why you were guided to take this action, but it made sense and you felt you needed to do it. The desire to take action likely came from your heart or gut rather than your mind. You knew that when you acted on this inspired idea it would make you happy.

Celebrate an inspired action you have taken in your life. Become aware of your inner guidance that aligns you with your inspired actions and how it communicates with you.

If you still need help aligning with your inspired action, you will find that there are infinite possibilities available to you when you approach taking action with curiosity and imagination. The questions you then need to ask yourself are: Which of these infinite possibilities is in highest alignment with what I am inspired by? Which is in highest alignment with my dreams and intentions? Which possibility makes me feel better inside than the others? Which possibility do I feel excited about? Listen to your body, listen to your inner voice—your intuition. Listen to your heart. What would you really love to do?

Be curious about the possibilities, as I was curious about engineering. Use your imagination! Imagine possible outcomes associated with the different actions you can take. Imagining the possibilities takes you beyond the solutions of your thinking mind. It takes you out of past known solutions, into the realm of the unknown. Listen to your heart. Listen to your gut. Trust that you, and only you, know what is inspiring to you. Your logical mind may try to convince you that you will fail by telling you that you are not good enough or worthy. Your logical mind will always try to protect you and keep you from stepping out of your comfort zone.

Imagine Stepping out of Your Comfort Zone

> *"Imagination is more important than knowledge. For knowledge is limited to all we now know and understand, while imagination embraces the entire world, and all there ever will be to know and understand."*
>
> ~Albert Einstein

Imagination provides you with an opportunity to explore reality beyond your thinking mind's limitations. When you are focused on your day-to-day responsibilities, there is no room in your brain for imagination. Sometimes, it's transformative to step outside of your thinking box and into the realm of "infinite possibilities" to give birth to the personal evolution you desire.

Imagination allows you to explore reality beyond everyday limits. To fully engage this capacity, we often need to let go of rigid thought patterns and adopt a curious mindset, similar to the curiosity we naturally embrace in childhood. When we are playful and open to new ideas, imagination becomes more accessible, transforming our perspective on what's possible. Just imagine what if without judging whether or not it could happen. Imagine what it would feel like if it could happen.

If that approach doesn't work for you, know that whenever you're listening to music, reading a book, or watching TV, curiosity is present, helping your imagination soar. It's the desire to seek out new knowledge to see the bigger picture. Curiosity is about learning new things. Has it been a while since you tried to learn or do something new? Is there self-doubt or fear when you think about stepping outside of your comfort zone? The phrase 'comfort zone' was coined by management thinker

Judith Bardwick in her 1991 work, *Danger in the Comfort Zone*: "The comfort zone is a behavioral state within which a person operates in an anxiety-neutral condition, using a limited set of behaviors to deliver a steady level of performance, usually without a sense of risk."

When you step outside of your comfort zone, your mind may find many excuses to try and stop you from taking action. You may feel stress or fear. Taking inspired action means that you may not have a complete roadmap at the start of your journey to achieve your desired outcome. This requires the confidence and courage to step outside of your comfort zone. You can't change your future unless you are willing to trust that everything will be as it is meant to be when you take inspired action.

Is your mind telling you that you can't do it based upon something that happened in your past? Is your inner child being reactive? Is there a limiting belief, past experience or something else creating an obstacle? Is it real? Is it true? What if? Imagine, what if that desired outcome is possible? Tap into your inner child and become curious about the possibilities. What emotions would you feel if that desire became a reality?

Maybe you don't know all of the answers. That's okay. I didn't know all of the answers when I planted the seed of creating the future through space technologies. All you need is to plant the seed and take a baby step in that direction to make it an inspired action. Don't let the limiting beliefs, doubts and fears hold you back from your destiny. As you take action, you build your confidence and courage. If you want to conquer fear, don't sit home and think about it. Go out and get started.

When you step out of your comfort zone, remember why you are taking that inspired action. Remember your intention, your desire, your dream. It might help to print it on a piece of paper and post it someplace you will see it every day to remind you and motivate you. Imagine how you will feel when you complete the intended action. Will you feel joy? Happiness? Excitement? The feeling is the motivation. The feeling inspires you to stay on track, to keep taking those inspired actions.

Yes, there may be challenges along the way. Yes, you will need to overcome the fear associated with stepping out of your comfort zone. There will be successes and failures on the journey. It's all worthwhile if you achieve your true desire. Think about ways that you will stay focused and positive about taking one step at a time, even if you don't know all of the steps needed at the start. Trust that even if you don't know now, you will know when it is time to take that step. There may be risks and costs to action. But they are far less than the long-range risks of staying in your comfort zone and not taking that action. With inaction, you may be missing the opportunity to live the life you were destined to live.

Taking Inspired Action Exercise

This inspired action exercise will provide practical steps that you can use to identify the inspired actions that are in highest alignment with your highest good in the present moment. In other words, the actions that will lead to the success and happiness that your heart desires.

Step 1: Recall how it feels when you take inspired action.

Think about a time in your life when you have taken inspired action. What were the feelings you experienced when taking inspired action in the past? Was there joy, excitement, a sense of knowing it was the right thing to do in the moment? Perhaps it was a decision you made that resulted in a positive direction in your life. Or maybe you committed to making a change that resulted in personal growth and happiness. The important thing is to remember how it felt in your body. Sometimes, it can feel like you are stepping out of your comfort zone.

Step 2: Make a list of inspired actions that you can take now.

Specifically, actions that are in alignment with the top three intentions you set in the last chapter. You are making an action plan for yourself to change your life to one you love living. This may require that you step out of your comfort zone. Your mind may try to tell you all of the reasons that you can't take that action, based upon your past experiences. These are the first steps to becoming the creator of your life. Remember, you don't need to know what all of the steps are now. Even just the first step is magnificent. It may be helpful to create an environment in which you can tap into your inner guidance:

- Quiet your mind. Allow yourself to explore the possibilities and truly feel: what if?

- Listen to music or find a relaxing place in nature or by the ocean, listening to the waves, where your only focus is on connecting with your heart and what you truly desire.

- Pay attention to any thoughts, feelings or images when you first awaken, before you open your eyes to start the day. This is likely your inner guidance communicating with you.

- Tap into the curious child within you and imagine the possibilities for the actions you can take now.

Step 3: Check-in with your body.

Your body is a source of inspiration and guidance. What is your body trying to tell you when you think about taking the action that you listed in Step 2? What are the sensations that you have in your body? Is there fear? Is there excitement? Is there tingling all over, or is there tension? Write down the sensations that you have for each of the possible actions in your list.

Step 4: Decide which inspired actions you are ready to take now.

Review your responses from Step 3 and decide which actions you can commit to taking now. Perhaps there are some actions that you will decide to take at a later time. Make a commitment to yourself and trust that you will persevere, you will overcome any challenges that arise along the way to your dream, your new reality. You will find the inspired action, step by step. Remember, no step is too small!

If needed, you can repeat this exercise when it is time to create more change in your life.

I didn't know how I would pay for college when I started on that path. I didn't know how or what it would take to someday be in a position to create the future and realize my childhood dream of working on technologies for space. I never imagined in my wildest dreams the possibility that I would someday lead an organization and make investment decisions for a $100M research and development portfolio. Miraculously, it all worked out as it was destined to be, step by step out of my comfort zone! With the **Power of Inspired Action**, I exceeded my imagined possibilities step by inspired step.

Next Steps

"Success seems to be connected with action. Successful people keep moving. They make mistakes but don't quit."

~ Conrad Hilton, Founder of
the Hilton Hotel Empire

You can do it! Keep moving forward to create your dream life, filled with success and joy. Just take the first step, even if it requires you to step outside your comfort zone. After all, your comfort zone is only your mind trying to keep you safe, based upon a past reality. You'll never grow and live to your highest potential unless you take some risk. Your mind will likely feel some anxiety and fear due to the uncertainty and unpredictability of forging a new path where you don't know all of the answers. However, don't let your mind stop you from taking action.

You don't need to know when you start where the journey will end. Trust that through the ***Power of Inspired Action*** you will know when you get there, step by step. Taking inspired action involves overcoming obstacles and listening to your intuitive inner voice. It's about stepping out of your comfort zone and taking one step forward at a time, even if you don't yet know all of the answers or where it will ultimately take you. Celebrate your successes by nurturing and honoring yourself along the way. Celebrate when you survive stepping out of your comfort zone (because you will, it was meant to be!). The best way you can celebrate your successes is with self-love and self-care, which we will discuss in the next chapter.

Chapter V

Power of Love, Part 1 - Cultivating Self-Love and Self-Care

> *"Love is the great miracle cure. Loving ourselves works miracles in our lives."*
>
> ~ Louise L. Hay, Author of
> *You Can Heal Your Life*

As I mentioned in the Introduction, Love—especially self-love—is the key to unlocking your power. When you embody love by feeling love in every cell of your being, you heal emotionally and physically. You have the power to create joy, abundance, and well-being. Self-love fuels this process, allowing you to become the creator of your life's journey.

In this chapter, you will learn about two very important things you will need to do to support yourself on the journey to become the creator of your life, and on the bigger journey called the game of life: self-love and self-care. As you take the inspired action steps on your journey you will need to confidently and courageously step out of your comfort zone. When you love and care for yourself, you are more committed to keep moving on your journey and overcome the challenges.

Self-love means treating yourself with the same kindness, compassion, and respect you give to others. It's an inner recognition of your worth, a feeling that you're enough just as you are, and it's crucial to creating fulfilling relationships. You can only give love to others that overflows from the love of self. Love for others emanates from the inside out. That is the way it was meant to be. Recall from Chapter III that our intentions create our reality. If you don't truly love yourself, you cannot truly be loved by others. It explains why my romantic relationships never lasted—I hadn't yet learned to love myself.

Do you love yourself now? Truly loving yourself means loving all of you unconditionally - including your body, your mind, and all aspects of your inner child.

Self-care is taking care of yourself; it replenishes your energy. It's another way you express love for yourself. Imagine your body is like the battery in your cell phone. Once your battery is discharged it must be recharged or your phone doesn't work very well. You are energy. You effectively have a battery that can be drained by giving more than you allow yourself to receive. Self-care is a conscious act you take to promote your physical, mental, spiritual, and emotional health. It is vital for building resilience toward life's stressors that you can't eliminate. When you've taken steps to care for your mind and body, you'll be better equipped to live your best life. This means allowing yourself to receive the same care you would give to others.

You cannot take care of others, just as you cannot truly love others, unless you take care of or love yourself first. I know from my experience, this is easier said than done. This point (self-love, self-care) really goes back to a theme I discussed in Chapter II. It involves making the shift from being externally focused to internally focused. Making the shift from only giving to others by allowing yourself to be on the receiving end of the loving and caring soul that is you. Making the shift from looking for love and validation outside of you to inside of you. Fully taking responsibility for your feelings at any *'now'* moment. Not relying on the judgements or opinions of others for validation. Being the sole creator of feeling loved and cared for from the inside out. Self-love and self-care results in emotional and physical well-being. You deserve it!

Self-Love

There was a time when I was more focused on being loved or liked by others, those people in my life at home and at work. I would say things that the people I was with wanted to hear, just to be loved by them. You might call that being a people pleaser. I was always judging myself based upon how other people judged me or how my mind perceived me to be judged. Perception is reality. When there is judgment, there is no love. The true meaning of love is unconditional.

When I was a child, my Dad would say terrible, mean things to me to try and get me to react. I learned to shut down my emotions. I learned to hold back any reactions, to hold back the expression of what I was truly feeling. I was effectively silencing my inner child, not allowing their voice to be heard. I remember when one of my boyfriends asked me: "Doesn't it bother you when your Dad talks to you like that?" I would just say: "No. I learned to shut my Dad out, to not let his words hurt me or cause me to react because I didn't like the consequences."

Unfortunately, to survive as a child, I allowed my external environment to control what I was feeling inside. I didn't know any other way to be. I didn't know that I had the power of being internally focused. The power to not be reactive to my external environment. In time, I lost the ability to access my true emotions.

I locked my feelings up in a box inside my heart. I locked my inner child behind a door, never to be heard from again until I learned the truth about what a terrible thing I had done. Now, I understand that self-love means embracing and allowing myself to feel any and all emotions that are rising within me. By setting my emotions free, I am embracing the whole of who I am, not just parts of me. I am lovingly allowing myself the freedom of expression.

Have you locked away any of your emotions? Do you allow yourself to feel what you are feeling?

In retrospect, my Mom was actually really good at this too. Maybe I learned it from her? I am sad that my Mom was never able to break free of her chains, never able to express her emotions until they erupted in a river of tears because they were overflowing and that was the only way for them to be released. Even when they erupted, she would judge herself for allowing her feelings to escape and the tears to flow. She had forgotten how to love herself.

Naturally, the same thing happened to me at work. I worked in a male dominated Aerospace and Defense career as an Engineer with less than 10 percent women. Early in my career, I was really concerned with how I was perceived by my male bosses. If a woman started crying about something at work, she was viewed as weak and unprofessional. She was labeled as being too emotional. At first, I would run to the Ladies Restroom to cry if I felt the tears coming. Then I learned to suppress my emotions at work, just as I had done with my Dad. I locked my emotions inside rather than expressing my truth, what I was truly feeling inside. Would you say that is loving to myself? No, I was not being loving to myself by keeping my emotions bottled up inside of me.

At the time, I didn't realize that I wasn't loving myself. There wasn't anyone to help me see the truth. It's not as if I hated myself, but I didn't feel worthy or good enough to give "love" to myself based upon my external world, based upon the judgements of those around me. I needed validation from the people in my life that I was worthy of love, because I didn't know how to love myself or why it was important. My ability to feel loved was completely externally validated. I was constantly judging myself and comparing myself to other people. I was worried about what other people thought about me.

Now I understand that each step away from my emotions was a step away from self-love. By embracing my inner child and honoring my emotions, I learned to replace self-judgment with self-compassion. The **Power of Love**.

Do you ever notice judgmental thoughts arising in your mind about yourself or others? The constant judgment and denial of emotions causes disease, it causes illness, it causes sadness at a deep level inside. Even though you might be able to maintain the façade of happiness to your external world, you likely have sadness deep down inside. When you fail to love and care for yourself, by suppressing your truth, your inner child becomes very sad. By refusing to listen to your inner child and the wide range of emotions they represent, they feel ignored, unloved, unable to be free, unable to feel joy.

One day while attending a leadership class, I realized the vast deep sadness that had been created inside of me. The teacher helped me to realize that there was a door in my mind that had been closed and locked. With my teacher's encouragement, I was able to unlock and open the door. When I opened the door, I discovered a sad, lonely little girl who had been locked up in the dark since I was a young child. The tears flowed and flowed down my face until I could cry no more.

How could I have done this to her? How could I abandon and lock up my inner child behind a closed door in my mind? Now I understand that my mind locked my feelings up because it was trying to protect me from things that caused me pain. Instead, all it did was create a deep well of sadness. I have forgiven myself and my mind for locking up my emotions. I didn't know my mind was trying to protect me, and I didn't know any better at the time it happened.

Now I understand the truth and I am committed to loving every aspect of myself. Every emotion, every aspect of my inner child is embraced with love and compassion. I have learned to accept myself as I am now. When I stopped judging myself by taking responsibility for my feelings and loving all of me, I became happier and eliminated the disease and pain in my body. I am perfect just as I am.

Do you truly love yourself? Do you allow yourself to receive the same level of love you willingly give to others, no conditions?

If you need to build self-love, consider these things. Self-love is not judging yourself. Self-love is allowing yourself to feel all of your emotions, no matter what they are or when they arise. It's about forgiving yourself for anything you ever said or didn't say, did or didn't do, and any judgment about self or others. Self-love is giving, but not to the extent that it drains your battery. It means nurturing yourself, all of you, whether you perceive it to be good or bad, wrong or right. Self-love is staying focused inside of you as much as possible, taking full and complete responsibility for how you feel about yourself. It's not basing how you feel on how others may judge or perceive you to be, or how others feel about you.

Self-love is removing your presence from negative people who don't support you. It's about only having loving people around you who do support you, have your back, and allow you to express your truth without you feeling judged by them in any way. Self-love is spending time under the moon and stars, the sun and nature. It's taking the time you need to sit silently and feel what is real for you in the '*now*' moment, embracing your emotions, embracing and nurturing your inner child. Self-love is being happy with yourself and connecting to your heart, knowing that you are perfect just as you are now. It's about rejecting people's false narratives and baseless theories about you. In other words, not accepting judgment from others in either your personal or professional life.

Be honest with yourself. Do you have some work to do to show yourself more love?

Self-Care

When I lost my right kidney at the age of 24, it was a wake-up call—a profound reminder of how crucial it is to care for my body. The experience changed everything, making me acutely aware of every choice I make, from staying hydrated to exercising regularly, to cutting out processed foods entirely. This commitment has been essential, especially knowing my family history. Everyone else in my family has battled heart disease at some point or is currently battling heart disease.

Watching them struggle with health challenges reinforced my commitment to a lifestyle that supports long-term wellness.

Unlike them, I haven't faced heart issues, and I believe it's because I've embraced the importance of self-care and self-love.

When you practice self-love and self-care you have the energy and emotional stability to be the best you can be. You can take on any challenge with compassion and love for self and others. Creating a healthy work-life balance is an essential ingredient in self-care. No matter how hard you push yourself, you will not achieve your highest potential in your career if you don't take care of yourself first and foremost.

By prioritizing self-care, you can reduce stress, enhance self-worth, and improve overall health. Simple acts of rest, exercise, and a balanced diet can significantly lower your stress levels and improve your overall health, as well as prevent chronic disease. The more you take care of yourself, the better you will feel about who you are as a person, thereby increasing your self-worth. Reducing chronic stress through self-care practices helps prevent health conditions like heart disease and hypertension (*APA, 'Stress effects on the body,' 2023*). Since I have prioritized self-care, I have significantly improved and maintained my overall health.

By practicing self-care, you can reduce opportunities for chronic stress, which can lead to chronic health conditions. When you take better care of your personal needs, you are better able to engage in healthy rather than dysfunctional relationships. This is partially due to the resultant increased self-esteem and self-worth that you feel. Your quality of life improves as a result of your overall well-being and sense of belonging. You have more energy and feel more energized in all that you do. Greater career success and abundance are created with ease and grace, because you are naturally more productive at work.

There are many possibilities available to help you in being more caring and loving to your body and mind. The key is to find something that works for you, something that you can commit to doing on a regular basis. To realize the benefits, it must become part of your regular routine. Consistency is critical.

Possible Self-Care and Self-Love Expressions

There are many ways to express love and care for yourself. Physical activity, relationship management and relaxation techniques all have benefits.

Relaxation Techniques:

- Meditation - Various studies indicate that meditating a consistent five minutes per day provides benefits, with at least 20 minutes per day resulting in lowered stress levels and improved health. I personally have found guided meditation to be very helpful. When I first started meditating, I couldn't get my mind to be still. Instead of being in the *now* moment, my mind would be wandering around thinking about either the past or future. I started using 10 to 20 minute guided meditations on the Insight Timer app when I went to bed at night. When I started participating in Dr. Sue Morter's free Monthly Healing Transmissions the last Wednesday of the month for one hour, I started to see and feel a shift in my ability to meditate. As with anything new, practice enhances your ability. While there are still times when I must ask my mind to be still, I can now meditate in stillness without the aid of a guided meditation.

- Watching TV - it could be as simple as taking the time to laugh by watching a comedy on television or on the computer.
- Listening to your favorite tunes on your music application or CD player.
- Taking time to stop and smell the beautiful roses or flowers.
- Spending time sitting in nature or doing something that brings you joy. For me, playing with my dogs brings me joy!
- Resting when you feel tired and need to recharge.
- Getting enough sleep.
- Using relaxation programs or apps regularly to incorporate meditation, muscle relaxation, or breathing exercises. There are a number of wonderful apps for meditation you can download for free, such as Insight Timer.

Physical Activities

- Exercising to keep your body strong. Jogging, walking, running, hiking, biking - there are numerous options. Even simple things like walking alone, with a friend or with a dog—I love walking my dogs!—provides huge benefits.
- Join a gym and commit to going there at least three times a week. This is actually a great way to get started because you have a monthly fee to motivate you!
- Weight training - In addition to cardiovascular exercises such as walking or running, it is extremely

beneficial to add weight training. You may want to consider working with a Personal Trainer initially until you are skilled at using the proper form to avoid injury. I have worked with a number of trainers over a 20 year period and learned a lot! Now, I have a very simple routine that I do in my home using a stability ball, a mat, and pairs of 10- and 20-pound dumbbells.

- Drinking at least sixty-four ounces of water to keep your body hydrated. With only one kidney, I tend to drink closer to my body weight in ounces of water!
- Eating healthy, whole foods, and avoiding alcohol, processed foods, and sugars.

Relationship Management - connection with other people and self is another way to nurture yourself.

- Nurturing your relationships with self, friends and family.
- Listening to what your body needs. Love your body. Your body is beautiful!
- Allowing yourself to be supported when you need support.
- Allow yourself to feel joy by doing things that bring you joy.
- Take time to recharge your battery when needed.
- Not allowing your mind to judge you. To love yourself means that you do not judge yourself and you do not allow yourself to be judged by others.

- Forgive yourself for anything you said or didn't say, did or didn't do.

- Maintaining a healthy work-life balance by including self-care practices in your daily routine. Commit to creating time for you! If needed, create self-care appointments on your calendar. You can do them before work, during lunch, or after work. Just do it for you!

- Treat yourself to a full body massage, a facial, or getting your hair done in a salon.

- Practice gratitude by reminding yourself daily of things you are grateful for. Write them down at night or replay them in your mind. Start your day, before your feet touch the ground, by being grateful for something in your life, even just waking up! Commit to having time to feel love and joy.

- Take time for vacation, including time to unplug from the demands of work and constant emails.

Yoga is a wonderful way to nurture your mind, body, and soul. I practice yoga at least three times per week. I highly recommend Dr. Sue Morter's BodyAwake® Yoga Membership classes. These are online-only yoga classes available through DrSueMorter.com / Morter Institute. While she offers live classes over Zoom twice a month, there are a plethora of recorded courses available at different skill levels and length with the membership. This is the link to a free class available on YouTube: https://www.youtube.com/watch?v=9_AJ9P9B098

"Dr. Sue Morter's BodyAwake® Yoga blends traditional yoga asanas (postures), breathwork, and energy medicine practices, resulting in a truly transformational practice that anchors your consciousness in the core of your body, activates your energetic circuitry, and awakens you to a new way of living." As Dr. Sue Morter says on her website, "There is a peaceful state of being running deep within the core. Allow that stillness to rise and flow. Allow it to direct the course of your life."

Many people, including myself, have found her BodyAwake® Yoga practice to be transformational. Even if you are not currently a yoga practitioner, you will experience tremendous benefits. I was always intimidated by yoga classes at the gym because my skill level was very low. With these classes, I am the only one that has an opportunity to judge my ability, and I know that judging my ability is not loving and caring. Since I started the practice five years ago, it has eliminated lower back pain issues and greatly enhanced my flexibility and overall strength. In addition to being transformative for my body, it has brought clarity and peace to my mind. Through the enhanced mind-body connection, I am better able to tap into my intuition—which I discuss in the next chapter—and listen to what my body is telling me.

Self-care means you allocate time to completely let go and recharge your battery. This means no checking or responding to emails when you're at the gym, out in nature, or on vacation. This means not checking emails while you're in bed, or before going to bed, or before taking care of yourself in the morning. Allow your mind time to be free of the demands of the external world. Your well-being and self-care should be your first priority. This means internally focused actions. The external demands can wait. They will still be there when you complete your self-care actions.

Self-Love and Self-Care Exercise

What will you do to practice self-love and self-care? In this exercise, you will develop a daily practice that you can use to develop your self-love and self-care. If you already have a practice, fabulous! By working through this exercise, you may discover changes you want to create in that practice, now that you have a new perspective on being the creator of your life. Turn on relaxing music if it helps to focus your mind. I know it always helps me!

Step 1: List the things you already do for self-care and self-love.

Include the frequency, time of day, and amount of time. For example, these are a few items on my daily practice list:

- Meditate every morning for at least 12 minutes.
- Celebrate and feel grateful for the things that I did for myself that are loving and caring—every morning I capture these things in a daily journal.
- Walk at least three miles every day in the morning at sunrise. This is accomplished with two walks—I have two rescue dogs!
- Do Body Awake Yoga for one hour at least three times a week before walking the dogs in the morning.
- Lift weights and stretch for one hour at least two times a week before walking the dogs.

Step 2: List the things you will commit to doing now.

This is your commitment to self-care and self-love for the new you. You can use the examples I provided at the end of the last section in this chapter (**Possible Self-Care and Self-Love Expressions**) or any other possibilities that are meaningful for you. Here are some additional examples:

- Once every two months I will take the time to have my hair done at a salon.
- I have my phone scheduled to enter "Do Not Disturb" mode from when I go to bed at night until I have completed my morning self-care routine.
- I am committed to taking time for a longer guided meditation (more than 30 minutes) at least one day every weekend.
- I make it a point to feel grateful and blessed everyday, especially for the beauty I see on my daily walks.
- Every day, at least once: I thank my body, I love my body, I tell my body it is beautiful.

Maybe you can't commit to doing all of the things you would like to do right now. Even if you plan to add more expressions of self-love and self-care to your life in the next month or next year, write down a timeframe of when you will start. As you can see, it doesn't need to be every day for each expression. Spending time out in nature or at the ocean could be a weekly or monthly expression of self-care. On the other hand, meditation could be a daily activity you choose to commit yourself to doing. Do commit to loving all of you everyday - mind and body!

Step 3: Review your list weekly or monthly.

Are you executing your plan? Do you need to make any changes to it? It's very important to look in the mirror and be honest with yourself. Remember to forgive yourself if you haven't met all of your commitments. More importantly, do not judge yourself based upon what you did or didn't do. Perhaps you were too ambitious in Step 2 about what you were committing to? If it is something you feel is important to start doing, be creative about when and how it could be included in your routine.

Step 4: Celebrate your successes!

Take time to be grateful for what you have accomplished. Cherish the moments that you are doing things that are internally driven, things that are loving and caring for you. Allow yourself to receive gratitude and love!

"As you are building your self-care and self-love plan, the following steps can be helpful" (Source: 5 Types of Self-Care for Every Area of Your Life -How are you caring for yourself today? By Elizabeth Scott, PhD, Updated on March 06, 2024):

1. ***Assess your needs:*** Make a list of the different parts of your life, and major activities that you engage in each day. Work, school, relationships, and family are some you might list.

2. ***Consider your stressors:*** Think about the aspects of these areas that cause stress and consider some ways you might address that stress.

3. ***Devise self-care strategies:*** Think about some activities that you can do that will help you feel better

in each of these areas of your life. Spending time with friends or developing boundaries, for example, can be ways to build healthy social connections.

4. ***Plan for challenges:*** When you discover that you're neglecting a certain aspect of your life, create a plan for change.

5. ***Take small steps:*** You don't have to tackle everything all at once. Identify one small step you can take to begin caring for yourself better.

6. ***Schedule time to focus on your needs:*** Even when you feel like you don't have time to squeeze in one more thing, make self-care a priority. When you're caring for all aspects of yourself, you'll find that you are able to operate more effectively and efficiently."

Next Steps

"Self-care is how you take your power back."

~ LALAH DELIA

I love this quote because it speaks to the heart of the issue. By over-giving and under-caring for yourself, what you are doing is giving away your power. There is no better time than now for you to take your power back by taking care of and loving yourself, first and foremost. Yes, it can be a mindset shift, a much needed and beneficial one. In Chapter VIII, I will cover the Power of Love, Part 2 - unconditional love and passion which can only be present with the Power of Love, Part 1: Self-love and self-care are essential internal elements to fully embracing the ***Power of Love*** in all aspects of being the creator of your life.

As you commit to self-care, envision how your practice will empower you to lead a fulfilling, joy-filled life filled with abundance. Embrace your journey with compassion, knowing that every step brings you closer to your authentic self. Imagine how much better your mind and body will feel now that you are loving and caring for yourself. Know and trust that you can and will do this for you! In the next two chapters, I will share two powerful tools that I have discovered on my journey to self-love and self-care: the Power of Music and the Power of Intuition.

Chapter VI

The Power Of Music and Sound

> *"Music does a lot of things for a lot of people. It's transporting, for sure. It can take you right back, years back, to the very moment certain things happened in your life. It's uplifting, it's encouraging, it's strengthening."*
>
> ~ Aretha Franklin

As Aretha Franklin states in her quote, "music does a lot of things." I have personally found music to be a very powerful and transformative tool in my life. It helps me to focus my mind when all my mind wants to do is chatter and distract me. I have experienced emotional and physical healing from powerful crystal bowl sound baths. I've also found that music can break down barriers and facilitate connection with others.

With the Power of Love, you committed to practices for self-love and self-care. If you haven't yet created your plan for self-love and self-care, take a few minutes now to go back to the practice discussed in the last chapter and capture your commitments to yourself in writing.

In this chapter, I will discuss the **Power of Music and Sound**. This is one of two powerful tools I have discovered that can transform your ability to implement self-care and self-love in your life: 1) tuning into the **Power of Music and Sound** to create focus, emotional and physical healing, and connection, and 2) the power of listening to your inner voice or intuition, which I will cover in the next chapter.

Power of Music and Sound - Focus

There were many times, in my past, when after a long day of work I would have trouble falling and staying asleep. All of the voices in my head would be incessantly reviewing what I had done wrong during the day. As I lay there desperately trying to sleep, my 'monkey mind' would be saying over and over: "You should have done this or you should have responded this way." The 'monkey mind' is the part of the brain most connected to your ego. It insists on telling you that you can't do anything right, it insists on judging you.

Since the ego has the ability to create false thoughts, it means that your mind is most likely not being factual about anything. Unfortunately, false thoughts are the inner chatter you hear most often. Does this sound loving to you? No, your mind is not being loving. Your mind is doing what it has been trained to do, your entire life, by your external environment—it's judging you! It's judging what you did or didn't do, what you did or didn't say. Have you had this experience in your life?

Have you ever had a challenge with your mind being still or quiet after a long, challenging day? Have the voices in your head judged you? Did your 'monkey mind' make it impossible for you to get the rest and sleep that your body needed? I feel your pain. Night after night this would happen to me! No matter what kind of day I had, my 'monkey mind' would make it very challenging to fall and stay asleep. If it wasn't about what had happened that day, it might be something that was scheduled to happen at work the next day. No matter how much I pleaded with my mind to be quiet, it wouldn't stop! I tried meditation, but even then my mind would not be quiet.

The only way I discovered that I could quiet my mind and get to sleep was to listen to music. Yes, music! Relaxing music—no words for my mind to focus on, only sound. Have you ever tried listening to music, or maybe even mindless TV at night to fall asleep? I discovered that listening to instrumental music gave my mind something else to do besides rehashing what had happened in the past or worrying about what would happen in the future. For years, this was the only way for me to reliably quiet my 'monkey mind' and get a decent night's sleep. While I am grateful and ecstatic that I no longer need the music to fall asleep at night, music remains a powerful tool in my self-love, self-care repertoire.

What are some of the ways I use music the power of music on my 'monkey mind'? In addition to using it to fall asleep at night, I often listen to instrumental, relaxing music during the day to help my mind focus on the task at hand. In fact, I used it when writing this book! Studies have validated that there are specific frequencies which help your mind focus. You can find quite a bit of this type of music on streaming services such as Apple, Spotify, etc. For most of the music applications you can do a search on "focus" music and it will suggest albums for you. A few of the many artists that I use are Steven Halpern, Yuval Ron, and Jeralyn Glass. Experiment to find which artists you resonate with the most. Don't be surprised if it changes from day to day.

There are many, many types of relaxing sounds to explore. I personally find that these sound frequencies help my mind to stay in the present moment rather than wandering off to the past or future. When I stay in the present or *now* moment and I am internally focused, I realize a state of 'flow.' This state of flow allows me to be more focused, productive, and efficient, thereby accomplishing tasks more quickly than I otherwise could. When you are in a state of flow you are effortlessly able to operate at peak performance.

Whenever I would travel for business, I would listen to music while doing work on the airplane. Not only would it help me to shut out the airplane noise, it would help me to feel relaxed and happy. It was amazing how much I could accomplish during the flight! If only I had been able to have the option to listen to music at the office consistently. Now that I work from home, I do have the option of listening to music while I am working. I have found the state of 'flow' to be especially helpful when I need to be creative. Do you listen to music and allow it to relax you often enough?

I also found that listening to music on the way to and from my work site provided significant benefits. On the way to work, I could focus on what I intended to accomplish that day, such that I could be more focused and productive once I arrived at work. On the way home, it was a way to decompress from the trials and tribulations of the workday, transforming my state-of-mind from work mode to self-care mode in the time it took to drive home. In addition, I also found that it made the drive time pass more quickly, and I was much less reactive to and stressed by traffic issues.

I have found that music helps me to get in the 'flow' with whatever I am doing. Have you ever listened to music at the gym? When I attended spin (cycle) classes at the gym, great music was the difference between an awesome and so-so workout. Magically, I felt stronger when pushing the pedals to a tune I loved to hear and sing along to. When I lift weights at home or at the gym, I find that I feel stronger and more motivated when I am listening to music I enjoy. The time just flies by. The right music can definitely motivate you to work harder without noticing that you are doing so—peak performance!

Power of Music and Sound – Physical and Emotional Healing

An emerging area of research in the medical and health care community is the power of music to provide physical and emotional healing. Numerous studies have shown it can reduce symptoms of pain and disease in the body. While there have been a limited number of formal studies performed to date, many musicians and doctors have seen the power that music can have on healing cancer in the body. Your body is much more powerful than you might imagine it to be when it comes to self-healing.

When my Dad had Alzheimer's, he couldn't remember who my Mom was and that she was his wife. While he could still remember that I was his only daughter, he thought my Mom was a caregiver I hired to take care of him. One day we were riding in my car and I tuned into the 'Frank Sinatra' station because they played music he used to enjoy when I was a child. It was amazing to me that someone who couldn't remember his wife of 60 years could still remember the words and sing along to songs on the radio that he had sung so many years ago. It was beautiful! I was surprised and delighted to see he was calm and happy being magically transported back in time through the old familiar sounds. For a short while at least, it brought him joy.

Music supports physical and emotional healing by helping you to remove energy blockages in your body. Whether you know it or not, you are energy! Within your body, there are seven energy centers, or Chakras. These Chakras (Image 03) affect your physical and emotional well-being. (Image source: Meditation Lotus Flower by Beetpro on Pixabay) Each Chakra, or energy center, in the body is associated with a color, a musical note, and a vibrational frequency (Image 04). The frequencies, known as the Solfeggio Frequency, are a set of ancient musical tones that hold special significance in terms of emotional and physical healing. While initially used in Gregorian Chants dating back to the 11th century, the Solfeggio frequencies were rediscovered in the 1970s, with scientific studies finding evidence of healing properties and positive impact on the body and mind.

The Seven Chakras or Energy Centers

Chakra	Note	Color	Frequency, Hz
Crown	B	Violet	963
Third Eye	A	Indigo	852
Throat	G	Blue	741
Heart	F	Green	639
Solar Plexus	E	Yellow	528
Sacral	D	Orange	417
Root	C	Red	396

Chakra Notes, Colors and Frequencies

Has music ever brought tears to your eyes? Think back to a time when a song brought you to tears—an unexpected, powerful release. That's music's unique power. When music touches your heart or soul, it's tapping into the emotions inside of you. While you may not be able to put your finger on the exact emotional response being triggered in the moment, know that it is happening for a reason. A good reason. The emotion being triggered needed a voice. It needed to be felt and embraced. If there are tears, know that a part of you is healing.

Every time I hear the song "Wildfire" by Michael Murphy on the radio, it brings tears to my eyes. I've heard that song 100's of times since 1975, and tears still stream down my face. The first time I heard a song with whales singing, it touched me so deeply that I cried. Sometimes it only happens the first one to three times that I hear a song, and sometimes it's enduring. Who you are physically and emotionally is always in a state of change, evolving and transforming. Your response to a stimulus can change based upon your emotional state in that present moment. It's beautiful and amazing how healing music is for your body and mind!

Has music ever made you want to get up and move? Have you ever had a tingling sensation or goose bumps all over your body when you hear certain music or move to certain music? If you have, then your body is speaking to you! Your body is saying, "Yes! Yes! Keep moving! Movement is what I need." Movement moves the energy in your body. Dancing to music improves your heart health and overall well-being. Music can be energizing and physically stimulating, releasing anxiety and tension in the body, if only you let it work its magic on you!

Just like listening to music, sound baths also have healing effects. A sound bath is an experience where you are immersed in deep sound vibrations. These vibrations are at specific tones and frequencies (Image 04), and they have the ability to heal by addressing energy imbalances in the energy or Chakra centers (Image 03). While different types of instruments can be used, I personally have enjoyed sound baths with crystal singing bowls as created by Jeralyn Glass. As stated on her Crystal Cadence website, "Crystal Singing Bowls are sound healing instruments made only with the highest grade of quartz crystal, which is guaranteed to be over 99.99% pure."

The alchemy singing bowls "are infused with gemstones, earth substances, and minerals such as imperial topaz, charcoal, morganite, turquoise, citrine, and precious metals like platinum and 24 carat gold." You can find many examples of Crystal Cadence sound baths focused on a variety of sound benefits through Jeralyn's YouTube channel, or in most music applications. With good headphones, the sound can work its magic! Better yet is discovering opportunities to experience a sound immersion or sound bath experience in person.

I attended a workshop in Arizona that included two 90-minute sound baths by Jeralyn Glass. Wow! My experience was that those sound baths felt amazing and transformative, seemingly transporting me to another world. She played a symphony of crystal singing bowls and chimes. There were also gong sounds. The sound immersion vibrated in every cell of my being. It allowed me to release emotions that were locked deep inside the energy centers in my body.

My mind had no choice but to be still, feel, and observe. Tears flowed down my face as the energy shifted in my body. My whole body physically vibrated as I allowed the music to guide me to releasing and healing. The sounds guided me to embrace and unlock emotions that had been locked up inside of me since I was a child. I felt as if I had been transformed into a new body and mind, a new me. It was essentially as if my mind and body had been rebirthed. There was no longer any pain in my body. The experience was a fabulous example of the power of sound to heal at an emotional and physical level! I highly recommend this type of experience.

If you would like to learn more about the emotional and physical healing power of music, I highly recommend this book by Jeralyn Glass (2024) - Sacred Vibrations: The Transformative Power of Crystalline Sound and Music.

Power of Music and Sound – Connection

In addition to emotional and physical healing, music can connect us to others in a magical heartfelt way. As Ella Fitzgerald said: *"Music is the universal language... it brings people closer together."*

Have you ever been to a live musical performance or concert? Do you remember what the energy felt like? Maybe it was an intimate jazz or classical music performance in which people tend to stay seated, yet you can see and feel the subtle movements in the audience members. Perhaps it was a rock and roll concert in a large stadium or arena where everyone is on their feet dancing and singing to their favorite songs. Talk about energy! Everyone in the audience is magically connected through the musical sounds of the performers on the stage. According to Marilyn Manson: "*Music is the strongest form of magic.*" I agree!

Music connects us to one another through the simple act of joining hearts to sing or listen to a song. Music was one of the things that formed a connection between my husband and I on our first date. Music is a topic through which there is either common ground and alignment or not. After all, it's not easy to hide when you don't enjoy a musical genre. We went to see the jazz band The Rippingtons on our first date because we both loved their music before we met. Through the music of The Rippingtons, we created and now share many beautiful stories and memories. We saw them play on our honeymoon near our home, and traveled numerous times to Newport Beach, California to see them play at the Hyatt Regency's Jazz Concert series in the summertime.

When my husband and I were dating, there were certain songs we would hear on the radio that we both resonated with and became "our songs" or our musical group—Hiroshima's "One Wish," and Gato Barbieri's "Europa." He and I also both love Steely Dan and Led Zeppelin. If we could only have one album on a deserted island, it would be the album *Aja* by Steely Dan. Music connects us to the people in our lives through our heart and soul.

Don't forget nature when it comes to sound. Yes, the power of the sounds of nature. Yet another connection, in this case between our heart and nature. I don't know about you, but I love the sound of the waves crashing against the shore whenever I am near the ocean. It brings me joy and peace, and stills my mind. The peaceful, beautiful serenades of the whales. The laughter and joy of the dolphins at play. The sound of the wind through the trees on a windy day, with each tree having its own unique song. The sound of rain or the powerful sound of a waterfall or stream. The sounds of so many different birds: the melodic and sometimes humorous sounds of the woodpecker, the sound of a hawk in the sky above elegantly soaring on the air currents, the songs flocks of birds sing while frolicking through the trees, and many more. The hum of a beehive or crickets. All of these sounds and more connect us to this beautiful planet earth on which we live.

Finally, the sound of complete stillness, a sound inspired by nature. As Eckhart Tolle said: "True intelligence operates silently. Stillness is where creativity and solutions to problems are found." Yes, stillness, the state when your mind is clear and quiet. The state where you can clearly hear and connect to your inner voice, your heart of hearts. Stillness requires being completely and wholly focused internally.

Stillness is the divine and devotional state of self-love and self-care. I encourage you to take time, at least a few minutes every day, to experience and connect with the stillness within you. You may be surprised by what you discover when you do so. I personally find that the biggest challenge with experiencing stillness is quieting my mind. With practice, you will find that achieving that state of mind becomes easier. In the beginning, you may need to ask your mind to be still. The key is to be patient and loving with your mind. Most likely, your mind is not accustomed to being still. Gradually build up the amount of time you spend in stillness as you learn this valuable skill. Your mind will adjust if you are persistent and loving.

Power of Music and Sound Exercise

In this Power of Music and Sound exercise, I will provide suggestions on how to connect with and embrace this power to support you on your journey.

Step 1: Identify the ways you currently experience the Power of Music.

Music is such an integral part of my life, I imagine most people listen to some music every day, but maybe not. This step is for making an assessment of your current state. Make a list on your computer, on a piece of paper, or in a journal reflecting on your current state for each of the items below. (Note: Leave space after each item to list the things you will do going forward for Step 2.)

A. When and how do you currently listen to music?

B. Is music used to help you focus your mind either for sleeping or exercise or while working to achieve a state of flow?

C. Do you currently use music to support physical or emotional healing? If so, to what extent?

D. Are there times when you listen to music to connect with other people, whether that is attending a live music event or sharing music with others in your home?

E. How much time do you purposefully take to experience stillness?

F. Do you ever allow yourself the freedom to express yourself by moving to music? List some examples.

Step 2. Identify the changes you will make to embrace the Power of Music more fully.

Based upon the information that I have shared about the Power or Music and Sound, consider how you will create more joy and love in your life through music. You can make a commitment to listening to music every day. Consider spending at least five to ten minutes in complete stillness at the beginning, end, or middle of your busy day. This can be combined with a time to listen to your intuition. You can choose to listen to the sounds of nature everyday as part of your daily routine—this can be done while you exercise by taking a walk outside or going on a hike, or just sitting outside in a park observing nature. You can also decide to quiet your 'monkey mind' by listening to music while you fall asleep at night or while you drive to work.

- For each of the items that you identified as your current state in Step 1 (your responses to A through F), assign a number one to ten. This number represents alignment with your desired future state. A 'one' equals 'Not Satisfied at All,' with a ten being 'Completely Satisfied.'

- For each of the items, list any changes that you will make to enhance and achieve your desired state of satisfaction. For example: Decide if you want to include movement to music and how you can make that a reality. Maybe it's while you are exercising. Recall past shared musical experiences and the joy they brought to your life. Find more ways to leverage the ability to connect through music.

- If it would help, you can also set an intention for bringing more of the **Power of Music** into your daily life, even if it is as simple as listening to music in the car.

Step 3. Explore a wide range of music and sounds frequently.

With the advent of digital music and mobile applications such as Apple Music, Pandora, and Spotify, you have a plethora of musical choices available to you. I encourage you to step out of your comfort zone from a musical perspective. Enjoying a wide range of musical sounds results in a greater opportunity for growth enhancing your creativity. Musical genres that I have found particularly helpful are: electronic, new age, smooth jazz, worldwide, and ambient.

- Observe how your body and mind react to different types of music. Make note of any music to which there is a physical or emotional response. Observe how that response changes from day to day. As you grow and evolve, your response may change.

- Notice when the music puts you in a state of 'flow' - a state in which you feel highly involved and focused on what you are doing, completely absorbed. Your mind is quiet and you create with ease. Learn to leverage your 'flow' state to achieve peak performance.

Next Steps

> *"To live is to be musical, starting with the blood dancing in your veins. Everything living has a rhythm. Do you feel your music?"*
>
> ~ MICHAEL JACKSON

This quote by Micheal Jackson speaks volumes. Through the Power of Music he had an enormous impact on the lives of many people worldwide. Through his deep commitment and dedication to his art and his vision for a better world, he always spoke and operated from a place of love and compassion. He was an honorable example of strength and courage speaking up about the need to overcome racism and take care of our planet; a twentieth century icon who changed the world through his music, love and compassion. Can you feel the music that is dancing through your veins? I feel it every day, and I feel blessed for the abundance of joy and love it brings to my life.

The Power of Music is one of two powerful tools for creating a life filled with love and joy. I hope that you will make music a bigger part of your life now. After all, according to quantum physics, humans are made of sound and light! In the next chapter, you will learn about the power of tapping into the sound of your inner voice, your inner light—the ***Power of Intuition***. Perhaps the power of your intuition is yet another form of the **Power of Music and Sound**?

Chapter **VII**

Power of Intuition - Listening to Your Intuitive Inner Voice

> *"Your time is limited, so don't waste it living someone else's life. Don't be trapped by dogma, which is living with the results of other people's thinking. Don't let the noise of other's opinions drown out your own inner voice. And most important, have the courage to follow your heart and intuition. They somehow already know what you truly want to become. Everything else is secondary."*
>
> ~ STEVE JOBS

This quote really resonates with me. It's so easy to let the opinions of others, your external environment, drown out your inner voice. Intuition is that quiet inner voice, an instinct that speaks directly to your heart and gut, guiding you toward choices that align with your true authentic self. Have the courage to listen to that voice and take action.

In this chapter, I will discuss the **Power of Intuition**. I have discovered that the Power of Music and the Power of Intuition can transform your ability to implement self-care and self-love in your life. In fact, I encourage you to listen to relaxing instrumental music while you read this book!

You may have heard the expression "Trust your gut," which is another way of saying trust your intuition. As a female Executive, I know that I often relied on and trusted my gut. In fact, studies show that 62 percent of Business Executives often rely on gut feelings. That means leveraging your intuition is more than something women do; successful men have also learned how to trust their intuition! In my role as a Technology Development Executive, I often relied on my intuition when making decisions about which technologies were in highest alignment with our future business needs. I learned to trust that gut feeling and rely on it to guide me.

Intuition means paying attention to how you feel about something, the inner knowing, inner truth. It doesn't come from the mind. It is found in the gut, in the heart. You have three brains: *the mind, the heart, and the gut*. Most people have forgotten that they have more than one brain and only listen to their mind. Intuition is not something to be ignored. Your mind will tell you that it knows better. Your mind will tell you that the only choice is a logical choice based upon what worked in the past.

Do you trust yourself to use your intuition? Have you ever regretted not listening to your intuition? I know I always regret not listening to my intuition. My intuition has supported me in making important decisions both professionally and personally.

I am a rescue dog Mom! When my big bad beautiful Bella (an 80 lb Doberman/German Shepherd mix I rescued at six months old) tore her Canine Cruciate Ligament, I faced the dilemma of listening to my intuition or trusting my dog's vet. According to the vet, a $5000 Surgery was the only way to heal her leg so that she could return to normal activity. After hearing this news, I thought to myself that I would pay anything to make her feel better and heal because I loved her so very much.

Then, the vet said that surgery would require them to cut the bone in her leg and put in a piece of metal to hold the leg together. Ouch. If that wasn't bad enough, Bella would need to be confined in a crate for eight weeks, completely immobilized! It would take at least six months before she could return to any normal dog activity, such as playing with Layla, the Doberman I rescued when she was ten months old. My intuition screamed out at me. My heart ached and my gut wrenched. Every fiber of my being screamed, "No!" There must be another way to heal my sweet, beautiful Bella.

That is when my dilemma began. Who do I trust? Do I trust the experienced vet, or do I trust my intuition? My logical brain and my husband said, "Listen to the vet, they are the experts, they know what is best for Bella. What are you waiting for? Do the surgery." But my heart was aching. You see, my Bella was a sensitive and beautiful soul. She slept by my side in my bed. She followed me everywhere when I was home and waited by the door patiently for my return when I left. She won't understand, she will feel like she is being punished. She loved going on walks and playing. Who do I trust? Myself or the vet?

My logical mind still didn't want to trust my intuition and told me to ask another vet. Well, I saw two other vets. They both said the same thing the first vet did. Surgery was the only way to heal my Bella. My inner voice was still screaming at me, "No! You can't choose surgery! You know what is best for Bella. Trust yourself." What if there was another way to heal Bella?

I then went to the only other source I had, Google. When I searched for a non-surgical solution, I discovered that the surgery the vets recommended increases the risk of dogs dying from bone cancer by 4000 percent! In fact, only 11 percent of dogs treated with this surgery return to normal limb function, due to complications from the surgery, including inactivity. Not a single vet mentioned these risks. Would you trust the vets that never talked about the risks? My intuition was right. Surgery was not the right answer for Bella. There was another way.

I found a lot of different braces that claimed to be an alternative for healing the injury. None of them intuitively felt like the right answer *until* I found the perfect brace. It didn't require a cast to get a good fit, and was flexible and adjustable enough to conform to Bella's leg and allow her to start walking right away. Imagine my joy when after only two and a half months with the brace, Bella was back to running, playing with and jumping on my other dog! I am so grateful that I trusted myself and listened to my intuition.

While you may doubt your ability to listen to your intuition, you have the ability to do so. Everyone does! Your inner voice is always speaking to you hoping you will listen. There are many possible ways that your inner voice will try to communicate with you. Not everyone hears their inner voice in the same way. I shared a personal example about how my inner voice spoke to me through my heart and my gut when it was time to make a very critical decision about my baby Bella.

When I was responsible for making important decisions about technology development and business development at work, I relied heavily on my inner intuitive voice. For investment or business pursuit decisions, I would say I relied more so on my gut feelings. In some cases, my boss would question my decision, asking me if I was certain we could succeed in my recommended path. While I often couldn't completely explain the rationale logically, I knew in my gut that it was the right path to pursue. Fortunately, my boss knew he could trust me to make the best decision for the company, and supported my recommended course of action based upon my past performance.

Think about a time when you were tapping into your intuition in either a work or personal situation. How was your inner voice communicating with you when you heard it speak to you? Was it through sensations in your body? Your body is communicating with you when you have these sensations. Where in your body did you feel the sensations? Was it in your gut, or in your heart, or both?

Did you feel tension? Did you feel contracted? If you feel tense or contracted, your intuition is telling you that is not the right path. If you feel expanded or there is joy when you think about pursuing that decision, then it is the right path.

When tapping into your intuition, it is important to focus internally and observe what is happening in your body. What are you feeling in your gut? Is your gut tight? Is it hard to breathe? Or, does your gut feel relaxed? Have you felt this before when making an important decision? What do you hear or feel when you listen to your heart? Does your heart ache as it did for me when I thought about the surgery for Bella, clearly steering me away from that decision?

Your inner voice might communicate with you through your emotions or feelings. How do you feel? What do you feel? Do you feel fear or sadness? Do you feel excited or happy? Do you feel energized? Do you feel drained? If you have access to your feelings, this may be the way your inner voice is providing guidance to you on your journey through life.

Maybe you hear your inner voice through your mind. When you close your eyes, do you see images or hear sounds? Some people are more visual and can receive guidance when they close their eyes. What images do you see? Is there a message from your inner voice in the image? What are the sounds or voices you hear, if any? What are they saying to you? Sometimes your mind can help you hear that inner voice by creating ideas, by imagining other possibilities. What ideas are you connecting to? What are you imagining?

Your intuition guides you toward what truly motivates and resonates with your highest potential. It identifies your blockages and suggests tools to break free from repetitive patterns that no longer serve you. It helps you recognize resistance, allowing you to differentiate between the limiting beliefs of your conventional mind and the insights of your intuitive mind. Enhancing your intuition involves discerning between fear-driven thoughts from your mind and those that emerge from love and joy. Intuition avoids imperatives like "You must do this," or "This is your responsibility."

You now have access to different ways that your intuitive inner voice can provide you guidance on your journey. The next step is to learn to trust your intuition by practicing and developing your intuition muscle. Your intuition wants whatever you value most, whatever is in highest alignment with your highest potential on your journey through life. Even though your logical mind feels it has the best decision for you, it may not bring you closer to your core goals or intentions. Listen to what your body is trying to tell you through its reactions. This is your inner voice, your intuition communicating with you.

Power of Intuition- Listening to Your Intuitive Inner Voice Exercise

You can use this Power of Intuition Exercise to tap into your intuitive inner voice for guidance. We talked about setting intentions in Chapter III. This is a time to set an intention for yourself to listen to and trust your intuitive inner voice by quieting the logical brain in following these steps.

Step 1. Create time and space to listen to your inner voice.

Set aside at least five to ten minutes during your day to translate your intuitive inner voice insights into actions and positive impact on your personal life and/or your business life.

- When you have a decision to make or it is time for change, this is the perfect time to check in with your inner intuitive voice.
- To activate your intuition, embrace the belief that all answers that are in highest alignment with your highest potential lie within you.

Step 2: Still your 'monkey mind.'

Close your eyes and take a minute or more to quiet your 'monkey mind,' quiet the chatter. If your mind tries to distract you, love your mind and ask your mind to be still. You can also listen to soft music to help quiet the mind.

Step 3. Breathe deeply into your gut.

Breathe in, breathe out through your nose. Make sure you are breathing all the way down to your belly and not just breathing up in your chest. You can even put your hand on your belly to feel it expand and contract. Relaxation is essential for this process.

Step 4: Listen and be curious.

Begin by asking yourself questions and listening carefully to your body, your mind, your emotions, wherever you tend to be able to hear that inner voice. Record the responses you receive or perceive in a relaxed state.

Step 5. Observe what you are feeling.

Open your awareness to what your body is trying to tell you. Your body is always trying to communicate with you. What is that intuitive inner voice trying to communicate to you?

Step 6: Trust and act.

The more you trust and take action, before you allow your mind to create doubt or reasons why you shouldn't act, the more your intuition will grow! It doesn't take any extraordinary abilities to access your intuition. You were born with the ability to do so. All you need is to learn to listen, trust, and act!

Next Steps

> *"When we decide to take back our own power, we discover that the true solver of problems is intuition, not reason."*
>
> ~ Deepak Chopra

As Deepak Chopra states in this quote, intuition is a powerful tool to solve the problems in your life. A problem could be as simple as making a choice. A choice between the possible solutions. The choices you make on your journey through life always have consequences. The better path is to listen to your intuition and ask for guidance when making your decisions, especially those that can be life changing.

If you would like a more easily accessible intuition exercise, I offer a complementary checklist on my website (subscribepage.io/pW5PkT): Tune Into Your Intuition: A Step-by-Step Checklist. Connecting with the power of your intuitive inner voice can be challenging, especially in high-stress environments. The checklist provides a six step process that guides you through practical steps to listen and trust your intuition effectively. The more you practice using your intuition the stronger it will become. Once you are skilled at tapping into your inner voice, you will be able to make decisions with grace and ease, knowing and trusting that you are acting in alignment with your highest good.

There is one final key to uncover on your journey: Embracing love and passion! In the next chapter you will learn how to find bliss, love, and joy in every aspect of your life. You will learn that Love is the answer, the key to unlocking the creator powers inside you. Without love in your heart, you can't sustain bliss or joy in your life. Love raises your vibrational frequency, allowing you to sustain bliss and joy. When you feel love flowing inside you, there is no fear, worry, or anger. You will learn why it is important to have passion in your life, and to follow your passion. Love and passion both start inside of you, and that is where you need to look to find it.

Chapter VIII

Power of Love, Part 2 - Embracing Love and Passion

> *"We are here to love each other. That is why you are alive. This is what life is for."*
>
> ~ Maya Angelou

This quote rings so true. We are here to be *love* in all that we do and create. Love is the answer. This doesn't mean that you love only certain people, or people who are always nice to you. This means loving all of life, even if there is no love in return. Love without conditions, unconditional love.

In the last two chapters you learned about two powerful tools—the power of sound and the power of your inner voice, your intuition. If you have not yet completed the exercises at the end of each chapter, take a few moments to do so now before proceeding.

In this chapter, I will share the secret power, the key that will unlock the power inside your heart, allowing you to fully express and live as who you came here to be, now! That secret power is embracing love and following your passion.

Love is the Answer, the Secret Power - The Key to Unlock Your Heart

Who knew it was so simple to create joy and abundance? Love is the answer. Love is not just about romance on Valentine's Day. Love is kindness, compassion, forgiveness, trust, possibility, precious, imaginative, joy, honesty, bliss, delight, and so many more things. It starts with being able to give and receive love from yourself, as we discussed in Chapter V. It's being able to stay in love when the world around you is inviting you into fear, worry, or anger. Love is the answer that will make your life and the world a happier and healthier place.

My life's mission is to become and live my life as the vibration of love. I only wish I would have realized the power of loving myself unconditionally when I was younger. My life would have been different if I had not been so reliant on feeling worthy of love based upon the people in my external world. The key to unleashing your creator powers inside is love, the secret weapon! It includes unconditional love for self and others. Love without conditions means embracing even those who challenge us, offering kindness and compassion without expecting anything in return. It includes being able to respond with love in the face of anger and judgment from others. It includes giving and receiving love.

Would not the world be a better place if everyone approached every situation in their life with love? Love is a secret weapon, because love can transmute all that is not love into love, if you only allow it the opportunity to do so. It transmutes fear, anger, worry, lack, sadness, and anything else that does not bring you joy into love. Your challenge is to maintain the feeling of love inside of you, no matter what happens in your external world.

To be crystal clear, I am not saying that you aren't allowed to let yourself feel other feelings. If other feelings arise inside of you, it is important to allow yourself to fully embrace them by allowing yourself to feel whatever is rising. Not allowing it to be felt only creates problems. Lovingly acknowledge the feeling, feel it and let it go. You have permission to cry a river of tears if that is what's needed to let it go. Only then can it be transmuted into love. Not allowing yourself to cry only keeps the feeling locked up inside, creating a space inside where you are not allowing love to be present. Love the part of you that is sad or angry, or whatever the feeling is that is present.

It has taken me until recently in my life to understand what the **Power of Love** truly means and to fully embrace the emotion of love. Looking back in my life, love has been a recurring challenge for me. Love was always the solution I was looking for whenever there was a challenge I needed to overcome. At a very young age, I created a box around my heart to avoid being hurt by others. Nothing could penetrate this box. I shut out the truth of how I felt. My emotions were verboten. When in the face of conflict, I either shut down or responded with anger and resentment.

Sometimes, it takes a surprising encounter to remind us of the power of love. Flipping through the pages of a local newspaper and seeing an adorable puppy that needed rescuing was the encounter that opened my heart up to love again. My business trip to St Louis had been canceled due to inclement weather. Instead of traveling, I had an opportunity to look at the local paper and saw the picture of an adorable six month old female Doberman/Shepherd mix puppy that needed to be rescued. My heart and my intuition said go see this dog. I hadn't had a dog since my first dog died at age eight, while I was going through my divorce almost 20 years earlier. It broke my heart when Magic, a female Doberman/Shepherd mix died while I was separated from my husband. I never had the opportunity to say goodbye to her.

When I went to the rescue open house and met this six month old puppy, my intuition said she was the one and it was time to open my heart again. Bella is a beautiful, loving soul! Almost everyone that saw her fell in love with her. This was Bella (see Image 05). The German Shepherd in her bonded to me and unlocked more barriers around my heart.

Beautiful Bella

This was the beginning of becoming a dedicated, loving 'Dog Mom.' Bella loved me every second of every day, no matter how I was feeling or what I was doing. Whenever I would leave the house, she waited patiently for my return. No matter how long I was away, she was ecstatic to see me when I returned, completely forgetting how sad she had been that I was away, forgiving me for missing her walks when I was out of town on travel, forgiving me for not being by her side all day because I needed to be at work or run errands. When I was home, she wouldn't even go outside unless she could share the time with me.

Living in a tall, skinny house near the beach with no real yard, Bella needed a playmate. This time I went to Dobies and Little Paws Rescue in Fillmore, California to find a purebred Doberman. Dobermans have a reputation for being vicious, but they are also 'velcro' dogs. 'Velcro' because they love to be close as if they are seemingly velcroed by your side. They thrive on love and cuddling. I rescued a ten month old female Doberman, Layla, who played well with Bella. She arrived at the rescue while I was there with Bella looking for her playmate. Layla's prior owners said they rubber banded her mouth shut to keep her from barking because they lived in an apartment. I was horrified and knew I was destined to save her. Due to the abuse she suffered as a puppy, she has always had anxiety issues. Even with the challenges, I am compelled to love her unconditionally. She opened my heart with her unconditional love for me.

It is so phenomenal to observe unconditional love with dogs. You can learn so much from your pets! Wanting Bella and Layla to benefit from having a yard to run around in inspired me to move to a house with a yard when they were about five years old. Bella and Layla were around eight years old when I was inspired to add another dog. It was perfect timing to bring in a puppy for them to play with, while they still had the energy. I was an avid follower on Facebook of the rescue where

I had rescued Layla. The rescue posted that they rescued a Doberman Mom and her litter of mixed breed puppies, which wasn't very common.

When I saw the picture of this adorable puppy, he called to me. My intuition said it was time and he was the one. I was blessed to be able to rescue him at eight weeks old! I had never had a male dog before and really wasn't sure what to expect. I named him Tiger. While the girls were not too happy about the new puppy, they soon discovered that there were benefits to having another dog around. Bella completely took Tiger under her care as a mother would. Scolding him, playing with him, teaching him about life and love. Truly beautiful!

Tiger is also a beautiful, loving soul. He loves to play a game with me before I take him on his walks. He sits on the couch and puts his paw in my hand, or both paws on my shoulders. While I gently caress his neck and chest, he licks my face with his ears back, staring lovingly deep into my soul, with his big brown eyes melting my heart into a bonfire of love, transmuting any feelings in me that are not based in love. Being a mix of Doberman, German Shepherd, Great Pyrenees, and a splash of wolf, he is a strong 100-pound male. Sometimes he will growl at me. I know he is communicating in the only way he knows how and I love him unconditionally. Just like he unconditionally loves me when I accidentally step on his paw. Dogs are the best teachers and bring so much joy into my life! If you own dogs, you no doubt understand.

Dogs are masters at unconditional love. One of the benefits of working from home now is that I can spend more time with my fur babies. My three rescue dogs have shown me how to embrace unconditional love. Only now can I say that "Love is the answer." I have transformed my response. I have awakened to love as the secret weapon for a life filled with joy and abundance.

Even though Bella is no longer physically by my side, she is forever in my heart. She is the first one who came into my life to teach me about unconditional love.

Bella also taught me about true passion. She was passionate about chasing cats, passionate about chasing rabbits, passionate about the need and desire for play time, passionate about going for a walk every day. I could see the excitement in her eyes and body. No matter how much her joints ached from her arthritis, she was always excited about doing what she was passionate about. She loved to lay down in the backyard with the sun shining on her, just being, sniffing the air and watching over her domain. Everyday things that she loved to do. She taught me that love is the answer.

You might be wondering how love can be a secret weapon at work. In my experience, it definitely is a secret weapon at work. Specifically, loving what you are doing at work and the people you most closely work with. Remember, I am not talking about romantic love. If you love what you are doing, you approach every day with joy and curiosity. You excel as a creator creating creations. You treat the people around you, the people you work for and with, the people that work for you, compassionately and respectfully. When there is love, everyone on the team is valued, supported, and has a voice and shared mission. Everyone learns, grows, and succeeds because they know they are appreciated and loved.

The teams I led at work would be characterized as high-performance teams. Each team member contributing a critical piece of the puzzle, working at their highest potential because they know they are supported and valued. During my corporate career, I had the opportunity to observe the actions and resulting performance of many other leaders and teams. I can state with certainty that when there is no love (open collaboration and compassion) present it is impossible to achieve success, because each person contributes as an individual rather than a piece of the whole.

Anyone who has watched a championship sports team or experienced an amazing concert knows that there are times when their performance is "out of this world". Everything is in the right place, at the right time or "in sync". In fact, all of the team members are communicating on an unseen energetic level in coherence. They instinctively know there is a "team energy" or a collective intelligence that enables them to excel. The creative capability of the whole working as one is exponentially higher than the individuals working in silos.

When there is love, there is collaborative creation, joy, and an abundance of success. My teams were able to successfully create things that had never been done before by sharing a common mission for creating success, imagining the possibilities, and trusting in miracles to happen. When we competed for contracts in this mode, we couldn't be beaten in any competition. We were revered and respected by our customers and the companies competing with us. Love at work is a secret weapon! Love is the answer!

Passion in Your Life

Passion is defined by the Oxford English Dictionary as *"an intense desire or enthusiasm for something."* Or, as one 2012 study in the journal Psychology of Well-Being describes it, a passion is a *"strong inclination toward a self-defining activity that people like (or even love), find important, and in which they invest time and energy on a regular basis."* For me, being passionate about something is equivalent to loving something. I love the feelings that I have when I am involved in that activity, whatever it may be.

If you don't know what you are passionate about, try tapping into your intuitive inner voice and listening. Ask yourself: "What am I passionate about?" If you still need help, there are resources available to you such as this free assessment: https://www.thepassiontest.com/the-passion-assessment

If the assessment doesn't resonate with you, another suggestion is to review Tony Robbins' "*10 Ways to Find Your Passion in Life*" article. Finding and knowing what you're passionate about in life is important.

Why is passion important? Passion motivates you to be the best you can be. Passion is what stirs you deep inside. It's the fire within that motivates you to be creative and committed to what you are doing.

Doing something you are passionate about brings more abundance, love, and joy to your life. When passion is missing, your actions lack meaning and you don't get the results you want. Passion is the seed from which your commitment blossoms! As Oprah Winfrey said: "*Passion is energy. Feel the power that comes from focusing on what excites you.*" Do you feel more energized and excited when you are doing something that you are passionate about? I know I do.

When I was a mentor as an Executive in a large Aerospace and Defense company, I would encourage all of my mentees to think about what they were passionate about doing or becoming. In my own career experience, I found that working on that which aligned with my passion for creating the future, motivated me to excel in my work almost effortlessly. The hard work was worth it because I was passionate about making a difference. It brought me joy to successfully create things that had never been done before.

Becoming and being a respected female leader in a male dominated environment because I was passionate about doing so also brought me joy. Since I was someone who could always see the big picture strategy, I was inspired to become the type of leader that helped others succeed in what they wanted to achieve by encouraging them to follow their passion. I found that most people working for me in Advanced Technology Development, or that I mentored, were passionate about creating the future.

For me, I have always been passionate about creating the future. As I shared in Chapter IV, when I was a child I had been passionately inspired and fascinated with *Star Trek* and other shows about space. Becoming an Electrical/Systems engineer at Hughes Space and Communications when I graduated from college provided me with opportunities to boldly go where no one had gone before.

Think about it. We wouldn't have DirecTV or Sirius Radio without the right satellite technology. It was a dream come true to be able to work on technologies and systems that would fly in space. It was a dream come true to be in a position to create the future for humanity. It lit me up inside and brought me joy. It ignited my curiosity! It inspired me, step by inspired step, to achieve Executive status as a Director responsible for a $100M Research and Development portfolio.

I am passionate about many other things too. I am passionate about music because it speaks to my heart and soul and quiets my 'monkey mind,' allowing me to be in 'flow'. I am passionate about quantum physics and neuroscience because it helps my logical mind understand that I am an energy being creating my life's experience. I am passionate about being an amazing dog Mom to my rescued fur babies because they give me an abundance of joy and unconditional love.

I am passionate about the fact that love is the answer because I have evolved so much by trusting in the truth of who I am and the power of love to transform and create possibilities. I am passionate about becoming the best I can be in this life through self-care and self-love by knowing that everything happens for a reason and it is good.

You can be passionate about any number of things in your life. The key is allowing yourself to pursue your passions. Don't deny that which truly excites you or brings you joy, for any reason. If it brings you joy, there will be love and abundance. Find a way to create that which brings you joy and excitement every day of your life. Love the life you are living, because you are the creator of your life.

It's likewise important to seek balance. Avoid activities that don't align with your true desires, and escape the cycle of distraction through temporary pleasures. Follow your intuitive inner voice to do what you love, whatever brings a genuine smile to your face. Take time to relax, live with less, and find joy in your journey. This way, you avoid wasting time trying to counterbalance dissatisfaction through harmful habits.

Embracing Love and Passion Exercise

If you haven't already done so, it is time to fully embrace the vibration of love and joy in your life. Again, this is not romantic love. It is a sensation in your body. It should be unconditional in nature. Unconditional love means that there are no conditions. If any conditions exist for you to feel this love, then it is not unconditional. Think about it as if you are tuning into a radio station. You are tuning into a specific vibrational frequency, the frequency of love. Love is the highest vibrational frequency you can feel, and it will lead to healing, abundance and joy. These are a few exercises to help you discover and embrace more love in your life:

Step 1: Write down experiences you have had in which you felt love.

Whatever it might be for you, write it down. You know the feeling. Here are a few questions to get you started:

- Was it a walk on the beach or watching a beautiful sunrise or sunset?
- Perhaps being out in nature or feeling the sun warming your body?
- Maybe it was spending time with a certain special someone or being close to your dog or cat?
- Was it listening to your favorite music or a bird singing?
- Was it the smell of the air after a rainstorm or seeing a rainbow?

Step 2: Consider and explore what might be limiting your ability to love.

Be curious about how you can be more loving to yourself and to others in your life. Consider the following:
- Have you been hurt by someone and unable to let go of that hurt?
- Are you afraid that if you allow yourself to love more that you will be punished or hurt in some way?

- Is there anything that makes you sad or angry when you think about love? Feelings of sadness, anger, fear, and pain can limit your ability to truly feel love.
- If any of these feelings are present, write them down. Think about what might have happened in your past that has made you feel that way now.

Step 3: For each of those items identified in Step 2, let go and forgive.

Forgiveness is about forgiving yourself and others for anything you said or didn't say, did or didn't do, for anything they said or didn't say, did or didn't do. We are all learning as we go in this game called life. Each past experience has contributed to the whole of who you are now.

- Embracing love means that you forgive.
- Embracing unconditional love means that there are no conditions for your love. You can't say, "I don't love you when you do that thing."
- Learn to express the feeling that you are trying to avoid feeling. Embrace that feeling and transmute it with love. Love is the answer. Know that everything happens for a reason.

Step 4: Commit to how you will be 'love in action' in your life by writing in down.

What does it mean for you to be 'love in action'? Here are some examples:

- It means that you are grateful for the things you have or have experienced that allow you to feel love and joy.
- Love in action is having compassion for others. Speaking and listening from your heart and not your thinking, critical mind.
- Speaking with compassion in the face of conflict will transmute all that is not love into love.
- It's about kindness, showing up in the world with compassion and acting for the greater good of all; meeting yourself and others with compassion and understanding in the present moment.
- Love in action is trusting that you live in a benevolent universe where everything that happens, happens for a reason. Trust that there is a reason for every experience you have, whether you perceive it to be good or bad. Be curious and imagine a positive perspective.

Step 5: Align with your passion.

Take a few minutes while listening to music to write down a list of the things that you are passionate about, using the statement: "I am passionate about…" For example, I am passionate about the power of sound.

- Once you have captured your passions in writing, put a star next to those things that are currently a reality in your life.

- For those items without a star, I recommend you become curious about how you can add them into your life.

- Capture any thoughts that arise about when or how you might be able to create more passion in your life. Baby steps are totally fine! Once you start the forward momentum toward the passion, it will magically become a reality for you. That is how powerful you are at creating your best life, a life that brings you abundance, joy, and love!

Next Steps

> *"Love transcends space and time. Its power can bridge hearts and minds. It has always been and always will be."*
>
> ~ Amy Leigh Mercree

Love does indeed transcend space and time. Unleash the power of your heart and let it shine upon your life. Love is the answer. Love is the key to unlocking the power in your heart, the power to create your life built upon a bridge between the heart and the mind. Love brings joy and miracles to your life. There are so many miracles around you, if you only take a moment to observe through the eyes of love. I have been fascinated and blessed by all of the miracles around me that I observe when I walk my dogs in the morning. The beautiful sunrise, the birds singing, the squirrels playing in the trees. So many miracles of life are there for you, if you take the time to open your heart and appreciate them.

This chapter covered the final critical key, embracing unconditional love and passion. By unleashing the **Power of Love**, you unlock your ability to create a life you love living where you have the power to be the best you can be. In the final chapter, you will reflect on your journey from start to finish. If you have followed the guideposts along the way, you are on a path to transform your life and ignite your happiness!

Chapter IX

Unleash Your Inner Powers - Love, Heal, Blossom and Create the Life of Your Dreams

> *"It's not about perfect. It's about effort. And when you implement that effort into your life, every single day, that's where transformation happens. That's how change occurs. Keep going. Remember why you started."*
>
> ~ JILLIAN MICHAELS

As Jillian Michaels says, it's really not about being perfect. There is no perfect answer. There is only what feels perfect for you in the present moment. Remember to not judge or compare yourself to others. Remember to look only inside for the answers you seek, with love. Congratulations! You made a commitment to yourself, to your well being, to living a joyful and fulfilling life filled with love. You have taken control of your life from the inside out!

By unleashing your inner powers, you have unlocked abundance, joy, and love. You are empowered to love yourself and love your life.

Reflection

Let's reflect on what you have accomplished on your journey of transformation and rebirth:

>**Chapter I** - You know your current mindset—maybe it is already starting to shift? You took the time to identify and write down your limiting beliefs and the significant past experiences impacting your current reality.

>**Chapter II** - You shifted your perspective from being the victim to one of cultivating a mindset of abundance and gratitude with the help of these insightful tools: 1. Shifting from being externally focused to internally focused with the Externally Focused to Internally Focused Exercise. This allows you to take responsibility for your life and shift from being driven by everything in your external world to creating your life from the inside out. 2. Overcoming Inner Child Wounds through loving and nurturing your inner child. You identified the aspects of your inner child that are being reactive to your external environment. You now have a tool with which to embrace, love and help your inner child heal from past wounds.

>**Chapter III** - You established a vision for your life, allowing you to manifest your desires. You

explored the power of having clear intentions and goals by writing them down. You have taken your power back. You now have goals and intentions to chart your course to living your life to your highest potential and creating a life of joy and abundance!

Chapter IV - You overcame any fears you might have had inside about taking inspired action towards your intentions and vision. You are prepared, ready, and willing to step outside of your comfort zone. You understand that there may be obstacles to overcome and you are ready for the challenge.

Chapter V - You learned the importance of self-love and self-care in creating lasting change. You identified ways in which you can be better at loving and taking care of yourself by creating and committing to a plan. No doubt you have already started doing some of the things in your plan. Remember to celebrate yourself! Celebrate that you are more loving and caring for yourself. You may find that the people around you respond positively to the changes you are making, and that you have more energy available in your battery to love and care for others.

Chapter VI and VII - You learned about a couple of powerful tools to assist you on your journey: the power of sound and the power of your intuitive inner voice to support you in loving and caring for yourself more. Are you spending more time listening to music and observing the impact it has on your mind and body? Are you finding that your 'monkey mind' has become more still? Are you starting to feel more joy in your life? Is it easier to make decisions every day when you listen to your intuitive inner voice? Is your intuition muscle getting stronger?

Chapter VIII – You learned and now understand that Love is the answer, your secret weapon. You understand that unconditional love for all includes compassion, forgiveness, and a lack of judgment. Love without expecting anything in return. You identified what you are passionate about. You have the tools to create opportunities for a more fulfilling life, filled with abundance, love, and joy.

While not explicitly identified as one of the Six Creator Powers, the **Power of Now** is a consistent thread through all of my recommended actions. The Power of Now means being *fully present in the now moment*. As Eckhart Tolle said in his book *The Power of Now: A Guide to Spiritual Enlightenment*, "As soon as you honor the present moment, all unhappiness and struggle dissolves, and life begins to flow with joy and ease. When you act out the present-moment awareness, whatever you do becomes imbued with a sense of quality, care, and love—even the simplest action." Your past experiences do not control you and do not determine your future, unless you let them. The most important time to be present in is the present moment, the infinite now moment where infinite possibilities exist.

If you completed all of the exercises suggested in the chapters of this book, you have ignited your inner light and are ready to be the creator of a life you love living. It is your destiny to be the creator of your life from the inside out. You are no longer a victim of your external environment. While it may feel a bit overwhelming, all you need to remember is the **Six Creator Powers** that flow through the stories and chapters in this book. These are the powers that support you in being the creator of your life. Unleashing these six powers will transform your life by igniting your inner happiness and love.

The Six Creator Powers

First, the **Power Inside**, by **shifting your focus from your external environment to internal**. Practice staying internally focused. Notice when you are focusing externally and shift back to inside of you. Rather than placing blame on what you can't control, take responsibility for your actions and your feelings. For many of the concepts I discussed, this is really the point. Leverage the Externally Focused to Internally Focused exercise whenever you are uncertain.

Practice knowing the feeling in your body and mind of being internally focused. It feels different in your body. Learn to listen to what your body is communicating to you. Focus on and love your inner child to reduce and ultimately eliminate reactivity to your external environment. Listen to your inner intuitive voice when making decisions or setting intentions. When finding your passion, remember to shift your focus internally. Make sure you can feel the passion inside of you, and that it is not being influenced by your external environment. Change your inner world and your outer world will change! You are the creator of your reality!

Second, the **Power of Intention.** It requires changing your paradigm and shifting to a more empowered and intentional mindset. Shifting your life from external validation to internal fulfillment. By embracing the feelings your heart desires, you can create a new reality filled with an abundance of love and joy, the life of your dreams. **Intention creates everything**! When you are clear on your intention, aligned inspired action happens with grace and ease. When you are focused internally, you are focused on the feelings and emotions you are creating on the inside. You are creating your external reality from the inside out, based upon the feelings you intend to create.

When you start the journey toward your vision for your life, you won't know every step that will be required on your journey. You set an intention for your first step. Once that step is completed, the path forward will become more clear, in divine right timing. Trust that you will know what is needed next, what that next intention will be when you get there. It may be hard to believe, but you will discover that is the truth.

Third, the **Power of Music and Sound**. If you have not already done so, add **tuning into** the **power of music** and sound to your life. Music is physically and emotionally healing. It helps you to embrace, release, or let go of the past. Music will help you to focus on the present *now* moment and quiet the 'monkey mind' from bringing up past experiences, memories that no longer serve your happiness and abundance. When you are internally focused, you can achieve a state of flow when listening to music igniting your creativity.

Music can help you to connect with the ***power*** of your ***intuitive inner voice***. Connect with nature by listening to the sounds in the natural environment around you and feel the inner peace that is created. Share the power of music with those you love and care about. Explore the power of music to create better relationships and connections with others. Allow your body to feel movement, inspired by the music you are listening to. Allow healing tears to flow down your face, if that is what is needed in the moment.

Fourth, the **Power of Intuition. Listening** to your ***intuitive inner voice*** in your daily routine to help you make the internal shift needed and make decisions with grace and ease, to live an empowered life that you love living! Your intuition guides you toward what truly motivates and resonates with your highest potential. The next step is to learn to trust your intuition by practicing and developing your intuition muscle.

Your intuition wants whatever you value most, whatever is in highest alignment with your highest potential on your journey through life.

While you may doubt your ability to listen to your intuition, you have the ability to do so. Everyone does! Most people ignore their inner voice. Learn how it speaks to you. There are many possible ways that your inner voice will try to communicate with you. Not everyone hears their inner voice in the same way. Listen to your body in addition to your mind. Don't let your mind override the wisdom of your heart and gut.

Fifth, the **Power of Inspired Action.** Ignite your inner light and creativity. Remember, there are infinite possibilities available to you when you approach taking action with curiosity and *imagination*. Imagine what might be possible. Don't wait until you think that you have every step planned out. The important thing is to take action, put things in motion. The path will emerge with every inspired action you take. It's okay to not have all of the answers at the start.

Yes, it may be a little scary to take that first step, but trust that you will know, and trust that you will grow, and learn, and gain confidence with every step. Overcome your fears by stepping out of your comfort zone. Trust that you will know what to do when you get there. Trust that the universe is supporting you on your journey to be the best you can be.

Sixth, **The Power of Love. Love is the answer! Love is the Secret Weapon** that will transform your life! Loving your inner child to overcome reactivity. Loving yourself unconditionally. Remember that being perfect is subjective and not objective. Love yourself even when you make a mistake. Know that you made the mistake for a reason, because there is a lesson to be learned. Do things for you, because you really desire to do them. Show yourself that you are loved, that you care about your well-being. Create more love in your life by loving and caring for yourself first. Love what you do by understanding and listening to your desires and passion.

When you live in alignment with your desires and passions, joy and abundance flow into your life with grace and ease. Listen to your loving heart when *listening to your intuitive inner voice*. Love your mind when it tells you stories. Love yourself by forgiving yourself for anything you did or didn't do, said or didn't say. Love yourself and others by not judging. Be heart centered in love in all that you do every day, personally and professionally.

I'll now share one more story to illustrate how the Six Creator Powers came together in my life experience. In this case, there were several career decisions that needed to be made. I had plateaued in my Executive role and it was clear growth opportunities were limited or nonexistent. My husband and I had also decided we would love to have a bigger yard for our dogs to play in. I had to decide between staying in my comfort zone in a known environment, or stepping out of my comfort zone and resigning from my position. After listening to my intuitive inner voice, I decided it was time to leave the big corporation. I chose to join a much smaller company and move to a new home with a bigger yard and a 20-mile commute to work.

At first, this new role was a dream come true. I realized my dream office location, one with an amazing ocean view. I was able to be near and see the ocean, which I was passionate about, every day at work. What could possibly go wrong? It was perfect! My role had me reporting directly to the Vice President as an Executive. While everything was amiable and professional when I began working there, I discovered that all was not as it had appeared to be from the outside looking in. The truth was that I was not valued or respected for my skills, experience, and contributions. In fact, there were many hidden truths. It was a toxic working environment for all except the favored.

What I didn't initially realize was that the toxic environment was affecting my health. When I went for my annual physical exam, the doctor said my kidney function was rapidly and dangerously declining. He suggested that I make an appointment with a specialist since I only had one kidney, having had the other one removed due to the fact it was polycystic and making me ill. Could the work environment really be impacting my kidney function?

While I was taking responsibility for myself by internally focusing, my body was telling me that this environment was not in alignment with my highest potential. Was the message that there is a better career choice for me now? The only choice I really had available at that point was to stay in this unhealthy environment or really step out of my comfort zone and start my own business. Which would you choose?

I considered my options: 1) I could stay in my dream office with a steady income, but that was making me sick because it was out of integrity with the truth of who I was; out of integrity with my values, or 2) I could step out of my comfort zone and resign to start my own business, not knowing how I would earn an income, hopefully recovering my health. I didn't really have anyone I could turn to for advice. My intuitive inner voice said listen to your body, listen to your heart.

It was clear my body was telling me it was time to take my next inspired action and reclaim my happiness and health. My heart said loving myself required self-love and self-care first and foremost. While I didn't have a clue about starting my own business or exactly what I would be doing, my intuitive inner voice told me that was what I needed to do; it was time for the next chapter of my life, which meant taking responsibility for my well being and starting my own business. My 'monkey mind' had many doubts. Yes, there were fears, there was uncertainty, there were limiting beliefs, there were many unknowns. Was I "good enough" to leave the security of a corporate position? Would I have enough or be able to earn enough money as a business consultant, or whatever I chose to become? I didn't know the answers.

I can now say that I chose the right path for me by resigning and starting my own business. In less than three months after my last day working in that toxic environment, my kidney function miraculously returned to normal! My intuition was right. The toxic work environment was not in alignment with my highest good. It was the best decision, and my destiny, to resign and start my own coaching and consulting business, to free myself from a job in which I wasn't appreciated or valued.

I listened to my intuition, it was time to keep moving forward one step at a time. Prioritizing self-care and self-love came with ease, because I had more time to do so. I overcame limiting beliefs by joining Toastmasters to become a better speaker and build my confidence in being good enough. There was more love and joy in my life from being able to spend more time with my dogs and in nature. I enhanced my connection to the power of music to help with physical and emotional healing. I enhanced my connection to my inner intuitive voice by taking the time to meditate and create stillness in my 'monkey mind.' I celebrated that I am the creator of my life and I alone had the power to change anything that wasn't making me happy. By taking responsibility for being the creator of my life, I had ignited my happiness and transformed my life to one I love living!

Loving myself first was the secret weapon to taking the inspired action needed to reclaim happiness and health. The challenge for me was being willing to step out of my comfort zone to create the change I desired in my life. By loving myself, I was able to trust that this was the best path for me. Everything covered in the prior chapters supported me in taking inspired action. Let's not forget the value of curiosity as well. The reality is that there are infinite possibilities available to you when you decide to make a choice about something, anything.

You always have guidance available to you. Your inner intuitive voice and your body know what is best for you. Listen to yourself. Listen to your body, your emotions, your heart and gut. Take time to be curious about how your decision feels to you in the present moment. It doesn't matter what anyone else thinks or believes. You are the only one with a vote when it comes to your happiness and abundance.

Is it scary to step out of your comfort zone? Yes, absolutely! When you turn that fear into excitement, you have shifted the perspective. It's only your mind or inner child that are afraid. Love the mind. Love the inner child. Help them understand that all is good, that what you are doing will lead to greater happiness, abundance, love and peace. The past is the past. All that matters is the present moment and what is best at this moment in time.

Next Steps

> *"The world as we have created it is a process of our thinking. It cannot be changed without changing our thinking."*
>
> ~ Albert Einstein

Your thoughts create your reality. As Albert Einstein observed, to change your reality requires a new way of thinking. It's time for you to shift from thinking with your mind alone to thinking with your heart and gut by unleashing your power. By changing my thinking, I have been able to unlock and ignite the hidden powers inside of me. I created the change I wanted to see by shifting my perspective. I am no longer the victim of my external circumstances by giving away my power. I blossomed into being the creator of my life from the inside out.

You are here to be the creator of your life and discover your magnificence by unlocking the powers inside your heart. Love is the answer. Love is the key that unlocks the creator powers in your heart. It's time now to shift your perspective to being the creator and loving your life. Unleash your creator powers by turning the key and unlocking them. Be the creator of your life from the inside out. Blossom into a life filled with joy, love, and abundance.

You have learned a lot on this transformative journey and have the practical tools needed to achieve your highest potential. On any journey there is change, and it is important to express gratitude for yourself and your commitment to being the best you can be in this game called life. Here are a few questions that will help you to celebrate your wins and create intentions to continue taking the next inspired action on your journey. It might be helpful to refer back to the lists you created in the exercises at the end of each chapter:

- What are some of the "ah ha" moments or revelations that you have had? No doubt there have been a few.

- Celebrate how far you have already come in shifting your perspective. Are you more aware of being internally versus externally focused, and how that impacts your energy and power? Are you motivated and inspired to become more internally focused, thereby becoming the creator of your life?

- Take a few moments to identify any wins you have already had in your life from the teachings and exercises in this book. This could be in your work or business, in your physical or emotional health, in your relationship with self or others. There are many ways in which the benefits can manifest themselves in your daily life.

- What is the one thing that has helped you the most, that you needed the most?

- What intentions are you committed to putting in place? These could be things you are continuing or things you will start doing, now that you have completed this book.

- What do you need to change to live your life with more passion and love?

I have provided a list of the references or resources that have been impactful in my life. I encourage you to explore these if you are inspired to do so. They will allow you to delve deeper into the powers discussed in this book.

Know that an observation is really a snapshot in time. It doesn't represent the whole picture. Know that your perception is your reality—you are the creator of your reality. Each of you has your own unique energy field that can be impacted and can impact others in your environment. And finally, understand

Love Yourself, Love Your Life

that you can use the principles and practices in this book to change who you are and gain access to more love and the infinite possibilities available to you. Creating the life of your dreams doesn't happen overnight. By continuing to unleash your inner power you will be empowered to love, heal and blossom into your highest potential.

I encourage you to continue to grow and evolve, using the tools provided in this book to create the life you desire. If you have any questions, would like to connect and learn more, or provide feedback, you can connect with me on Facebook (@ Gail Taylor-Smith), and LinkedIn (@Gail Taylor-Smith). You can also sign-up for my newsletter and receive a complementary step-by-step checklist to practice tuning into your intuition at subscribepage.io/pW5PkT. My passion is to do all that I can to elevate consciousness through these enduring principles. How will you think differently, now that you have ignited your happiness with your new awareness? You have the power inside of you to love yourself and love your life! Unleash your inner powers and create the life of your dreams! And so it is!

With gratitude and love!

References and Resources

1. Morter, S. (2020). The Energy Codes : The 7-step System to Awaken Your Spirit, Heal Your Body, and Live Your Best Life. Atria Books.
2. Find additional information about free meditations, courses, podcasts and Body Awake Yoga classes with Dr Sue Morter at: https://drsuemorter.com/
3. TUNE INTO YOUR INTUITION: A STEP-BY-STEP CHECKLIST available free on my Love Yourself, Love Your Life website: subscribepage.io/pW5PkT
4. Tolle, Eckhart (2000). The Power of Now: A Guide to Spiritual Enlightenment. New World Library.
5. Dyer, Wayne W. (2006). The Power of Intention. Hay House.
6. Dispenza, Joe (2013). Breaking the Habit of Being Yourself: How to Lose Your Mind and Create a New One. Hay House.

7. American Psychological Association. "Stress effects on the body", March 8, 2023 has more details about the effects of stress on the body
8. Learn more about Jeralyn Glass and the Power of Music:
    a. Glass, J (2024). Sacred Vibrations: The Transformative Power of Crystalline Sound and Music
    b. Crystal Cadence Website: https://crystalcadence.com/
    c. YouTube Channel: https://www.youtube.com/channel/UCeqJQkuTKj6u8ZiUAFGVC3w

Acknowledgments

My deepest gratitude to:

My wonderful mother, who always believed in me and encouraged me to follow my dreams. Thank you for always being there for me with understanding and support. Thank you for the sacrifices you made, and the strength and perseverance you demonstrated in your commitment to being a loving mother. Thank you for finding a way to keep food on the table, buy gifts for Christmas and birthdays, and provide what was needed to survive even if it meant that you would go without. The lessons I have learned from you have meant everything to me. I am so grateful to have you in my life.

My beloved rescued fur babies, Bella (German Shepherd/Doberman rescued at 6 months old), Layla (Doberman rescued at 10 months old), and Tiger (Doberman, German Shepherd and Great Pyrenees rescued at 8 weeks old) for showing me how to fully embrace and receive unconditional love. Being a dog Mom has brought me so much more than I ever could have imagined, beyond my wildest dreams. Thank you for speaking to my heart and soul when I saw you, letting me know we were meant to be together. I am grateful for all of the walks, kisses, cuddling, and abundance of joy you have given me, for which

I feel so blessed. You helped me to unleash my inner powers through your unconditional love and passion. You are and will forever be a part of me, in my heart of hearts with love.

Dr Sue Morter. I feel so much love and gratitude for all that you do and have created to share with your community. You opened my eyes to the loving soulful truth of who I am. Every experience has been transformative. As you continually evolve and uplevel, I continue to discover more of my magnificence and how to unlock more of my creator powers. Your LiveAwake and IGNITE programs ignited my creativity and provided the inspiration for me to write this book and share your magnificence as a way shower for others. I am blessed! Thank you also for the Energy Codes, monthly Healing Transmissions, Body Awake Yoga and Energy Codes Coaching Certification program.

The Energy Codes Community of beautiful souls for which I feel so much love and gratitude for all of the love and guidance you have provided. I am particularly grateful for the BEST practitioner sessions which guided me in finding and unlocking deeply buried wounded aspects of myself.

Jeralyn Glass and your amazing, beautiful and transformative crystal bowls and Crystal Sound Healing Oracle. Your ability to create healing sound has helped me to unleash and heal parts of me that were ready to be released and embraced. Your Power of Sound was the only thing that could connect and unlock hidden, wounded parts of me buried deep in my body and mind. So many tears. So much evolution. Thank you Jeralyn! Thank you also for guiding me to my own divine set of beautiful crystal bowls whose magical sound I cherish.

Steven Ringelstein. With heartfelt gratitude for guiding me to your Multidimensional Leadership program as was agreed to in our soul contract. It was my destiny to work with you in divine right timing. You started my journey of rebirth by showing me the truth. In Mayan cosmology you are my challenge and a gift, the White Mirror of truth. You opened my eyes to my true purpose and mission in this life. You helped me to see that judgement and acceptance are two sides of the same mirror. I am forever grateful to you.

My Toastmasters friends for all of your support and guidance in enhancing my communication, listening and speaking skills in a supportive and positive learning environment. I am grateful for your constructive feedback and all I have learned from you about creating and sharing personal stories.

My author coach and editing team from SelfPublishing.com for all of their support and guidance in creating the best possible experience for my readers. I am grateful for your sage advice in creating a best-selling book in which to share my experience and achieve my mission to help others unleash their inner power, embrace self-love, and blossom!

My body, mind and soul for all that they have done for me in this lifetime. My heart is filled with love and gratitude for all that you have done and all that you do every day to support me in this magnificent and magical game of life. Thank you for supporting me in unleashing my inner creator powers to love, heal, blossom, transform my life and fulfill my life's mission. I love you and you are beautiful!

Thank you, dear reader, for sharing this journey with me and unlocking your highest potential by loving yourself and your life!

About the Author

Gail Taylor-Smith, CEO of Taylorsmith LLC, is a dynamic leader, accomplished mentor, and passionate advocate for personal empowerment and professional growth. With an impressive career as a former executive for a large Aerospace and Defense company and a Technology Transition executive at a small Research Laboratory, Gail earned numerous leadership awards and a reputation for inspiring individuals and teams to achieve their fullest potential. She currently serves as the only female on the Board of Directors for Information Systems Laboratories, contributing her expertise to foster innovation and growth.

Combining her engineering expertise from UCLA (BSE) and USC (MSEE) with a passion for self-development and her experience as a loving dog Mom to three rescue dogs, Gail has dedicated over eight years to researching and mastering transformational practices. Gail has completed numerous self-development and leadership training programs, including the Center for Creative Leadership, and Multidimensional Leadership. A certified Energy Codes® Coach through the Morter Institute, Gail has dedicated herself to helping others transform their lives through self-love and personal development.

A proud Toastmasters International leader since 2018, Gail is an accomplished speaker that excels in inspiring others to find their voice and leads by example as a club President and Vice President of Education. In *Love Yourself, Love Your Life*, she shares her transformative self-discovery journey and proven tools to help readers unlock their inner power, embrace self-love, heal physically and emotionally, and create lives filled with joy, love, and abundance.

www.ingramcontent.com/pod-product-compliance
Lightning Source LLC
Chambersburg PA
CBHW060831050426
42453CB00008B/648